# Probabilistic and Biologically Inspired Feature Representations

# Synthesis Lectures on Computer Vision

Editors
**Gérard Medioni,** *University of Southern California*
**Sven Dickinson** *University of Toronto*

Synthesis Lectures on Computer Vision is edited by Gérard Medioni of the University of Southern California and Sven Dickinson of the University of Toronto. The series publishes 50–150 page publications on topics pertaining to computer vision and pattern recognition. The scope will largely follow the purview of premier computer science conferences, such as ICCV, CVPR, and ECCV. Potential topics include, but not are limited to:

- Applications and Case Studies for Computer Vision

- Color, Illumination, and Texture

- Computational Photography and Video

- Early and Biologically-inspired Vision

- Face and Gesture Analysis

- Illumination and Reflectance Modeling

- Image-Based Modeling

- Image and Video Retrieval

- Medical Image Analysis

- Motion and Tracking

- Object Detection, Recognition, and Categorization

- Segmentation and Grouping

- Sensors

- Shape-from-X

- Stereo and Structure from Motion

- Shape Representation and Matching

- Statistical Methods and Learning

- Performance Evaluation

- Video Analysis and Event Recognition

Probabilistic and Biologically Inspired Feature Representations
Michael Felsberg
2018

A Guide Convolutional Neural Networks for Computer Vision
Salman Khan, Hossein Rahmani, Syed Afaq, Ali Shah, and Mohammed Bennamoun
2018

Covariances in Computer Vision and Machine Learning
Hà Quang Minh and Vittorio Murino
2017

Elastic Shape Analysis of Three-Dimensional Objects
Ian H. Jermyn, Sebastian Kurtek, Hamid Laga, and Anuj Srivastava
2017

The Maximum Consensus Problem: Recent Algorithmic Advances
Tat-Jun Chin and David Suter
2017

Extreme Value Theory-Based Methods for Visual Recognition
Walter J. Scheirer
2017

Data Association for Multi-Object Visual Tracking
Margrit Betke and Zheng Wu
2016

Ellipse Fitting for Computer Vision: Implementation and Applications
Kenichi Kanatani, Yasuyuki Sugaya, and Yasushi Kanazawa
2016

Computational Methods for Integrating Vision and Language
Kobus Barnard
2016

Background Subtraction: Theory and Practice
Ahmed Elgammal
2014

Probabilistic and Biologically Inspired Feature Representations

Michael Felsberg

ISBN: 978-3-031-00694-4     paperback
ISBN: 978-3-031-01822-0     ebook
ISBN: 978-3-031-00079-9     hardcover

DOI 10.1007/978-3-031-01822-0

A Publication in the Springer series
*SYNTHESIS LECTURES ON COMPUTER VISION*

Lecture #16
Series Editors: Gérard Medioni, *University of Southern California*
                Sven Dickinson *University of Toronto*
Series ISSN
Print 2153-1056    Electronic 2153-1064

# Probabilistic and Biologically Inspired Feature Representations

Michael Felsberg
Linköping University

*SYNTHESIS LECTURES ON COMPUTER VISION #16*

# ABSTRACT

Under the title *"Probabilistic and Biologically Inspired Feature Representations,"* this text collects a substantial amount of work on the topic of channel representations. Channel representations are a biologically motivated, wavelet-like approach to visual feature descriptors: they are local and compact, they form a computational framework, and the represented information can be reconstructed. The first property is shared with many histogram- and signature-based descriptors, the latter property with the related concept of population codes. In their unique combination of properties, channel representations become a visual Swiss army knife—they can be used for image enhancement, visual object tracking, as 2D and 3D descriptors, and for pose estimation. In the chapters of this text, the framework of channel representations will be introduced and its attributes will be elaborated, as well as further insight into its probabilistic modeling and algorithmic implementation will be given. Channel representations are a useful toolbox to represent visual information for machine learning, as they establish a generic way to compute popular descriptors such as HOG, SIFT, and SHOT. Even in an age of deep learning, they provide a good compromise between hand-designed descriptors and a-priori structureless feature spaces as seen in the layers of deep networks.

# KEYWORDS

channel representation, channel-coded feature map, feature descriptor, signature, histogram

# Contents

# Preface

This book comes during a deep learning revolution in computer vision, when performance of, e.g., object classification on ImageNet [Russakovsky et al., 2014] has improved vastly from top-5 error of 26% in 2011 to 16% in 2012. The major paradigm shift has been to move from engineered image features ("pixel f***ing" according to Koenderink and van Doorn [2002]) to learned deep features. So why write this text now? Many recent publications making use of deep learning show a lack of rigor and their way to *throw data at the problem* is unsatisfying from a theoretical perspective. Attempts to put deep networks into established frameworks as done by Mallat [2016] are essential contributions to the field. Deep learning is very important from a practical perspective, but having a well-founded understanding of the underlying features and how they relate to common approaches can only help whether you are using deep learning or engineered features. Indeed, there might be a twist to use channel representations inside of deep networks, but there are further motivations to write this text. One reason is to honor the work by Gösta Granlund, the father of channel representations, who recently finished his academic career. A second motivation is to summarize one of my own branches of research, as I have been working on feature representations since my master's thesis 20 years ago (Felsberg [1998]). Last but not least, this text addresses many mathematical and algorithmic concepts that are useful to know and thus I want to share with students, colleagues, and practitioners. None of those groups of people is addressed exclusively and presumably none will see this as a primary source of information, but I hope that all will find new aspects and try to formulate new research questions as a consequence.

Michael Felsberg
April 2018

# Acknowledgments

My work and the topic of this book have been constructively influenced by many colleagues, but primarily I would like to name Gösta Granlund, former head and founder of the Computer Vision Laboratory at Linköping University; Gerald Sommer, my Ph.D. supervisor; my colleagues at CVL who contributed to this book's content in some way or another, Per-Erik Forssén, Reiner Lenz, Klas Nordberg and my Ph.D. students Erik, Fredrik, Johan, Kristoffer, and Martin; and my colleagues outside of CVL who contributed, Remco Duits, Hanno Scharr, Ullrich Köthe, Rudolf Mester, Kai Krajsek, Norbert Krüger, and Richard Bowden.

Besides fruitful scientific exchange with colleagues, research also requires funding, and the collected work here has been financed by a long list of projects. Since we have ongoing projects with all founding agencies that supported our earlier work, I simply name the respective still ongoing projects. This research was partly supported by:

- the Swedish Research Council through a framework grant for the project Energy Minimization for Computational Cameras (2014-6227);

- the Wallenberg AI, Autonomous Systems and Software Program (WASP) funded by the Knut and Alice Wallenberg Foundation;

- ELLIIT, the Strategic Area for ICT research, funded by the Swedish Government;

- the Swedish Foundation for Strategic Research (Smart Systems: RIT 15-0097);

- the EC's Horizon 2020 Programme, grant agreement CENTAURO; and

- Vinnova through the grant CYCLA.

Michael Felsberg
April 2018

# CHAPTER 1

# Introduction

Designing visual features has been a fundamental problem of computer vision for many decades. Visual features have to represent visual information in a suitable way, where the definition of *suitability* has been shifting regularly, resulting in various feature design principles. Also, after the recent progress of deep learning, and deep features, these principles are still relevant for understanding and improving deep learning functionality and methodology. A principled understanding of feature design is the basis for analyzing the lower layers in deep networks, trained on complex tasks and big datasets.

## 1.1 FEATURE DESIGN

Feature design principles are systematic approaches to design features and avoid ad-hoc solutions ("pixel f***ing" according to Koenderink and van Doorn [2002]). The idea behind visual features is to transform raw values from cameras and other visual sensors into some intermediate representation, the *feature descriptor*, that is more relevant to the solution of the problem addressed [Koenderink, 1993].

Historically, the design of feature descriptors has seen many changes. During the early years of computer vision, feature extraction has mainly been considered as an algorithmic problem, a sub-problem of artificial intelligence, within computer science [Papert, 1966]. Since then, computer vision has become an interdisciplinary field and feature extraction has advanced toward models influenced by physics, statistics, electrical engineering, mathematics, neuroscience, and cognitive science.

In this process, the interpretation of an image has changed from being a simple byte array to being a sophisticated object reflecting real-world properties including models for point-spread functions and lens distortion, noise and outliers, continuous signals with sampling and interpolation, perspective transformations, and reflectance modeling. Even the interpretation by observers is sometimes reflected in feature extraction, e.g., by non-maximum suppression and local inhibition, adaptivity, and structural completion. Still, all features are based on digital image information and need to be computed in a digital system taking into account computational and memory resources.

Visual features are usually considered as part of some *hierarchical processing scheme*. Already in the work of Marr [1982], visual information undergoes processing in several steps, starting at the primal sketch (basically feature extraction) and ending at a 3D model representation. Later, hierarchical models split the feature extraction into several levels, low-level features such as edges and lines, mid-level features such as corners and curvature, and high-level features such as object outlines, before considering constellations and geometric information [Granlund and Knutsson, 1995, p. 8]; see Figure 1.1.

In this process, the concept of *locality* emerges and leads to nested frames [Granlund and Knutsson, 1995, p. 9] arranged in a hierarchical way; see Figure 1.2. Moving higher up in the hierarchy increases the effective support of the local operation and increases the level of abstractness by removing irrelevant information, or "stripping off context" as formulated by Granlund [1999].

The same principle is applied to the layers in a deep network. At each layer, a local operator is applied to the sub-sampled output of the previous layer, leading to a growth in effective support in the original input image [Goodfellow et al., 2016]. In this way, a sequence of operators with limited spatial support eventually covers the whole image. In deep networks this sequence contains nonlinear operations, but the principle itself also applies to linear operator design [Mallat, 2016] and nested local operators, or operator networks, replace complex and more global operators [Felsberg, 2002, p. 120].

The researcher who chooses a feature descriptor has to consider many possible feature designs and different attributes, some of which are listed in the preceding paragraphs. The researcher who wants to analyze and understand the learned features in a deep network has to choose an interpretation frame, some kind of model that forms the basis of interpretation. Even the neuroscientist has to choose a model to interpret measurements made in a biological system. In any of these cases, feature models are useful knowledge, and the purpose of this text is to introduce the reader to one specific approach, the model of *channel representations*.

## 1.2   CHANNEL REPRESENTATIONS: A DESIGN CHOICE

Channel representations are a particular design choice for feature description. They are general, work in different dimensions, e.g., images and sequences, with sparse and dense data, and for vector valued data, e.g., color images and flow fields. In some cases they are superior to other methods, in other cases they might be inferior, but just the fact that one and the same programming library can be used in all cases is a major advantage. For this purpose, a link to relevant code repositories is `https://github.com/micfe03/channel_representation`.

In a nutshell, channel representations fuse the concepts of histograms and wavelets and are characterized by combining advantages from both frameworks. In particular (see also Figure 1.3),

- they are multi-dimensional,

- they apply soft-assignments, and

- they obey algebraic constraints that enable reconstruction.

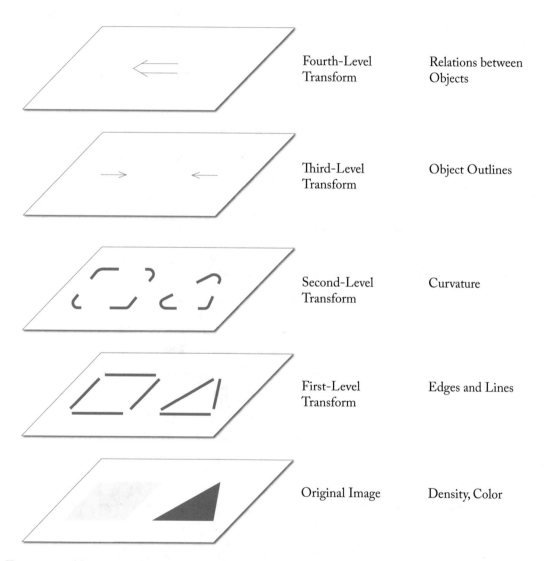

Figure 1.1: **Abstraction hierarchy based on** Granlund and Knutsson [1995, p. 8].

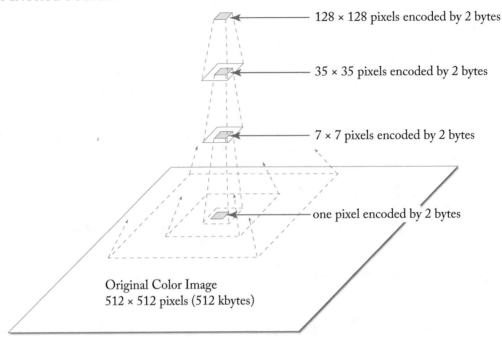

128 × 128 pixels encoded by 2 bytes

35 × 35 pixels encoded by 2 bytes

7 × 7 pixels encoded by 2 bytes

one pixel encoded by 2 bytes

Original Color Image
512 × 512 pixels (512 kbytes)

Figure 1.2: Nested frames based on Granlund and Knutsson [1995, p. 9].

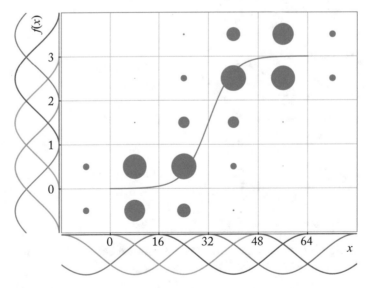

Figure 1.3: Example for the channel representation of a real-valued 1D function $f(\cdot)$, encoded in spatial $(x)$ and value $(f(x))$ channels in a 6 × 5 grid. The size of the dots in the respective cells represents the channel coefficients.

All these aspects will be considered in detail in the subsequent chapters. After introducing some basics of feature design, channel coding, and channel-coded feature maps (CCFMs) will be introduced. In the subsequent chapters, the decoding and visualization of feature maps will be discussed as well as their probabilistic interpretation. Each chapter is concluded with a short summary.

CHAPTER 2

# Basics of Feature Design

In order to define channel representations and to describe their properties, some terminology and concepts need to be introduced, which is the purpose of this chapter. Channel coding is based on local operators, whose design is guided by statistical properties (accuracy, precision, robustness) and geometrical properties (mostly invariance or equivariance). Algorithmically, it is a dense or sparse, grid-based approach, combining histograms and signatures. It is well motivated by biological observations.

## 2.1 STATISTICAL PROPERTIES

In practice, the input of any operator has to be considered as noisy and the input noise is propagated to the operator output. Thus, the operator output has to be considered as an estimator of the ideal result and potentially suffers from bias, errors, or outliers. More formally, these terms are defined as follows.

The *bias* (systematic error) of a visual feature may occur at different levels and often has severe effects. For instance, structure-tensor based corner detectors such as the Harris detector [Harris and Stephens, 1988] have a tendency to move the location of the corner toward the interior, although this can be mitigated by a correction step [Förstner, 1991]. Also, high-level features such as ellipses are often extracted using algorithms that suffer from bias [Kanatani et al., 2016]. Note that the bias of a feature reduces its *accuracy*, i.e., the proximity to the true values, and has to be distinguished from the variability of the estimator, i.e., its *precision*.

The *variability* of a visual feature is a measure of random errors, repeatability, or reproducibility. A feature with high precision shows a small variance of the output in comparison to the variance of the input, but it still may suffer from low accuracy. Typically, experiments for assessing the feature extractor confuse the effects of systematic and random errors by using the root-mean-square error (RMSE), i.e., measuring mean deviations from the ground truth [Rodehorst and Koschan, 2006]. If no ground truth is available, often only precision is assessed and systematic errors are neglected [Schmid et al., 2000]. Furthermore, visual feature extraction might be prone to *outliers* and including these in the precision measurement might lead to unbalanced results.

The *robustness* of a visual feature is a measure of the insensitivity to violations of model assumptions. If some model assumption is violated, the operator output might become random and (quadratic) precision measures are dominated by the resulting outliers. However, the operator itself or some subsequent step might detect the outlier and thus avoid further use of the spurious result.

Therefore, it makes sense to evaluate precision and robustness separately, e.g., as done in the visual object tracking (VOT) benchmark [Kristan, Matas, Leonardis, Vojir, Pflugfelder, Fernandez, Nebehay, Porikli and Čehovin, 2016]. A typical measure for outlier removal in feature extraction is the coherence of the structure tensor. The first eigenvector of the tensor represents the local signal orientation if the difference of first and second eigenvalue is large. The double-angle vector is an integrated representation of this principle [Granlund and Knutsson, 1995].

The tensor representation is still limited as it cannot represent two independent orientations, even if they co-exist. In general, the same local data can be subject to multiple mid-level interpretations, which leads to the concept of *metamery*, as introduced by Koenderink [1993], where metamery describes the ambivalence of the stimulus (icon) for a given feature descriptor (N-jet).

In order to represent multiple orientations, a mid-level representation with more degrees of freedom than the structure tensor is required. As explained by Granlund and Knutsson [1995], the structure tensor can be computed from a minimal set of three filters with a $\cos^2$-shaped angular transfer function and increasing the number of angular transfer functions directly leads to the concept of channel representations; see Chapter 3. Before we take this step, we will look into other terms, in particular invariance and equivariance, that are relevant to the development of structure tensors.

## 2.2  INVARIANCE AND EQUIVARIANCE

The example of the structure tensor for signal orientation estimation establishes also a prototypical example of the invariance-equivariance principle. If the image is rotated, the eigenvalues of the structure tensor remain the same (invariant) and the eigenvectors are rotated by the same angle as the image (equivariant).

Unfortunately, in literature the term *invariant* is often used without proper definition. Obviously, it is not enough to require that the output is not affected by a certain operation in the input space because this has a trivial solution, an operator with constant output [Burkhardt, 1989] that lacks separability [Mallat, 2016].

Also, the often used example of shift-invariant operators by means of the magnitude Fourier spectrum is problematic as it maps many completely different inputs to the same equivalence class; see Figure 2.1. This figure illustrates different contours that are all described by the same magnitude Fourier descriptors [Granlund, 1972], but they are obviously not related in shape.

Actually, the proper definition of invariance is more complicated than simply requiring constant output or global symmetry [Mallat, 2016]. Mathematically, it is more straightforward

Figure 2.1: Illustration of faulty extension of equivalence classes under invariance formulation: contour of a pedestrian (left) and two contours with the same magnitudes of Fourier descriptors (center and right). Illustration from Larsson et al. [2011] used with permission.

to define *equivariance* [Nordberg and Granlund, 1996], [Granlund and Knutsson, 1995, p. 298]:

$$f(\mathbf{A}y) = \mathbf{A}'f(y), \qquad y \in Y. \tag{2.1}$$

Here, $f : Y \rightarrow X$ is an operator (feature extractor), $\mathbf{A} : Y \rightarrow Y$ a transformation on the input space, and $\mathbf{A}' : X \rightarrow X$ the corresponding transformation on the output space. Technically, the two transformations are different representations of the same transformation group and there exists a homomorphism between them.

The equivariance property is also called strong invariance [Ferraro and Caelli, 1994], left invariance [Duits and Franken, 2010], or covariance [Mallat, 2016]. In contrast, $f$ is called invariant under $\mathbf{B}$ if

$$f(\mathbf{B}y) = f(y), \qquad y \in Y, \tag{2.2}$$

which might, however, result in too large equivalence classes for elements in $Y$ or lack of separability, as pointed out above. In the literature, this is also referred to weak invariance [Ferraro and Caelli, 1994] or right invariance [Duits and Franken, 2010].

In deep learning literature, the two terms are often not kept distinct. Shift-invariance is used for both, the convolutional layers (refers to equivariance above) and max-pooling layers (refers to invariance above, Goodfellow et al. [2016]). In practice, the most useful feature representations establish a *split of identity*, i.e., a factorization of the output into invariant and equivariant parts [Felsberg and Sommer, 2001].

In what follows, invariance and equivariance will be kept as separate concepts, but note that equivariant features often behave invariant under scalar products, i.e., they form isometries.

A necessary condition for obtaining invariant scalar products is that the output space of the operator $f$ establishes a tight frame, i.e., the generalized Parseval's identity applies. In certain cases, this can only be achieved approximately due to effects of the pixel grid and deviations from the invariance property can be used to optimize discrete operators on the grid.

For instance, the Scharr filter Scharr et al. [1997] has been optimized by minimizing the anisotropy of the structure tensor. Note that different assumptions in the formulation of the scalar product and thus the weights in the optimization lead to different results and the Scharr filter might not be the most isotropic choice [Felsberg, 2011].

Further practical problems besides grid effects are caused by the final extent of image data. Global scale-invariance can only be achieved if data is available on an infinite domain. Since this is impossible in practice, the image domain has to be extended by other tricks, e.g., periodic repetition (Fourier transform) or reflective boundaries (discrete cosine transform, DCT) of a rectangular domain. However, these tricks hamper a proper rotation invariance. Using a circular domain with reflective boundaries theoretically solves all issues, but becomes infeasible to compute [Duits et al., 2003].

## 2.3    SPARSE REPRESENTATIONS, HISTOGRAMS, AND SIGNATURES

Obviously, useful features need to be feasible to compute. Depending on the application, the selection of features might be limited due to real-time constraints and this is actually one area where deep features are still problematic. Also, the space complexity of features, i.e., their memory consumption, might be decisive for the design. In the past, paradigms have shifted regularly back and forth between using compact features and sparse features [Granlund, 2000a].

The kernel trick in support vector machines (SVMs) and Gaussian processes are examples of implicit high-dimensional spaces that are computationally dealt with in low-dimensional, nonlinear domains. In contrast, channel representations and convolutional networks generate explicit high-dimensional spaces. The community has conflicting opinions in this respect, but recently, compactification of originally sparse and explicit features seems to be the most promising approach, also confirmed by findings on deep features [Danelljan et al., 2017].

Another strategy to improve computational feasibility and the memory footprint is to use feedback loops in the feature extraction. Whereas deep features are typically feed-forward and thus mostly do not exploit feedback, adaptive [Knutsson et al., 1983] or steerable [Freeman and Adelson, 1991] filters are a well-established approach in designed feature extractors. In relation to equivariance properties and factorized representations, adaptive filters often exploit projections of the equivariant part of the representation, e.g., orientation vectors or structure tensors.

Alternatively, iterative methods such as diffusion filtering can be applied [Weickert, 1996], which potentially open up more efficient feature extraction using recurrent networks. The relationship between recurrent schemes and robust, unbiased feature extraction has been identified, for instance for channel representations Felsberg et al. [2015]. In that work, also the connection to population codes and their readout [Denève et al., 1999] has been made explicit.

Channel representations and population codes combine properties of a signature-based descriptor with those of a histogram-based descriptor; see Figure 2.2. Signature-based descriptors, e.g., speeded-up robust features (SURF) and 3D SURF as proposed by Bay et al. [2008] and Knopp et al. [2010], respectively, consist of an array of feature-values[1] indexed over coordinates. Histogram-based descriptors, e.g., bag of visual words (BOV) and fast point feature histograms (FPFH) as proposed by Sivic and Zisserman [2003] and Rusu et al. [2009], respectively, contain the cardinality (counts) of feature-values in dictionaries or histogram bins.

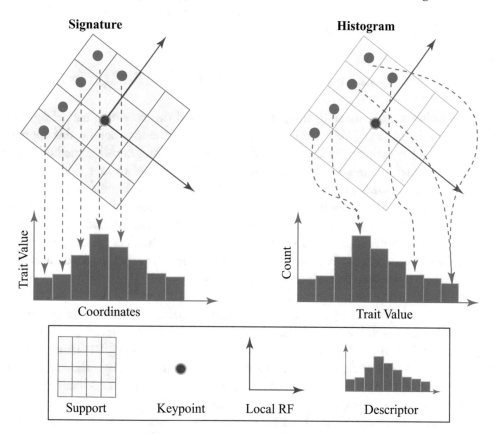

Figure 2.2: The two main classes of descriptors: signatures and histograms (here in a local 2D reference frame, RF). Figure based on Salti et al. [2014].

In this text, the main difference in the use of histograms and dictionaries (visual vocabularies) is that the former are regularly placed in some space, whereas the latter are irregularly

---

[1]In their terminology, Salti et al. [2014] refer to traits for what is called feature elsewhere in this text.

clustered. Histogram- and dictionary-based descriptors often suffer from the lack of spatial information, which is most commonly addressed by spatial pyramids, e.g., for BOV [Philbin et al., 2007]. However, according to the same authors, dictionary-based descriptors also suffer from quantization effects that have a major effect on their performance.

This problem has been addressed in Fisher vectors (FV) that move from dictionaries to Gaussian mixture models (GMM), which also estimate sub-bin displacements and variances [Sánchez et al., 2013]. Similarly to FVs adding displacement estimates for irregularly placed models, channel representations add displacement estimates to regularly placed histograms, most apparent in the formulation as P-channels [Felsberg and Granlund, 2006]. The regular spacing of channels makes a separate variance estimation unnecessary. See Chapter 3 for the technical definition of channel coding.

## 2.4    GRID-BASED FEATURE REPRESENTATIONS

Based on the observations made in the previous sections of this chapter, channel representations belong to the class of *grid-based feature representations*. The idea behind this approach is to compute a density estimate of the feature distribution by histogram-like methods. In machine learning, density estimation by histograms is usually referred to as a *nonparametric approach*, in contrast to parameter fitting for a known family of distribution, e.g., normal distribution [Bishop, 1995]. A hybrid between those parametric approaches and histograms are mixtures of parametric models, e.g., Gaussian mixture models (GMMs), and kernel density estimators (KDEs). The drawback of GMMs is the relatively demanding parameter estimation by expectation-maximization; the drawback of KDEs is the relatively slow readout of density values, as the kernel needs to be evaluated for all training samples.

Thus, despite their success in machine learning, GMMs and KDEs are too slow to be used as feature descriptors. Instead, grid-based methods such as histogram of oriented gradients (HOG, Dalal and Triggs [2005]), the scale invariant feature transform (SIFT, Lowe [2004]), and distribution fields (DFs, Sevilla-Lara and Learned-Miller [2012]) are successfully used, e.g., in multi-view geometry (point matching) and visual tracking. They are of central importance to visual computing and have in common that they combined histograms and signatures. This is achieved by computing local histograms over the spatio-featural domain, i.e., a 3D domain consisting of 2D spatial coordinates and one orientation (SIFT/HOG) or intensity (DF) coordinate. Consider the case of DFs: the image is *exploded* into several layers representing different ranges of intensity; see Figure 2.3.

Whereas DFs make an ordinary bin assignment and apply post-smoothing, channel representations apply a soft-assignment, i.e., pre-smoothing, which has shown to be more efficient [Felsberg, 2013]. The channel representation was proposed by Nordberg et al. [1994]. It shares similarities to population codes [Pouget et al., 2000, Snippe and Koenderink, 1992] and similar to their probabilistic interpretation [Zemel et al., 1998] they approximate a kernel

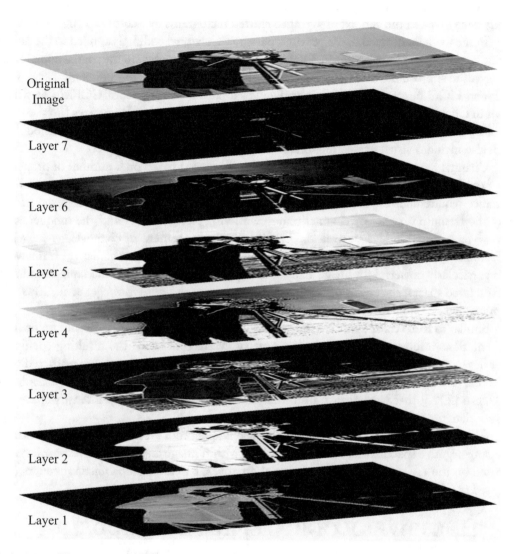

Figure 2.3: Illustration of DFs: the image (top) is *exploded* into several layers (here: 7). In each of the seven layers, intensity represents activation, where dark is no activation and white is full activation. Each layer represents a range of intensity values of the original image. The bottom layer represents dark intensities, i.e., the high activations in the bottom layer are at pixels with low intensity in the original image. Each new layer above the bottom one represents, respectively, higher intensities. In the seventh layer, the high intensity pixels of the original image appear active. Figure from Öfjäll and Felsberg [2017].

density estimator in a regular grid [Felsberg et al., 2006]. The mathematical proof has basically already been given in the context of averaged shifted histograms by Scott [1985].

In the work mentioned in the previous paragraph, channel coding is applied to the feature domain, i.e., as a histogram approach. Obviously, it can also be applied to the spatial domain, i.e., as a signature approach. Combining both results in CCFM [Jonsson and Felsberg, 2009]. Both SIFT and HOG descriptors can be considered as a particular variants of CCFMs, as will be shown in Chapter 4. The CCFM framework allows generalizing to color images [Felsberg and Hedborg, 2007a] and its mathematical basis in frame theory enables a decoding methodology, which also includes visual reconstruction [Felsberg, 2010]; see Chapter 5.

Channel representations have originally been proposed based on a number of properties (non-negativity, locality, smoothness; Granlund [2000b]). These properties together with the invariance requirement for the $L_2$-norm of regularly placed channels [Nordberg et al., 1994] imply the frame properties of channel representation [Forssén, 2004] and the uniqueness of the $\cos^2$-basis function [Felsberg et al., 2015]. Irregular placement of channels, as suggested by Granlund [2000b], obviously does not result in such a stringent mathematical framework, but is particularly powerful for image analysis using machine learning and the representation of less structured spaces, such as color. In that sense, color names [Van De Weijer et al., 2009] can be understood as a non-regular spaced channel representation.

Similar to RGB color-space and intensity space, the non-negativity constraint for channel representations implies a non-Euclidean geometry. More concretely, the resulting coefficient vector lies in a multi-dimensional cone and transformations on those vectors are restricted to be hyperbolic [Lenz et al., 2007]. This also coincides with observations made by Koenderink and van Doorn [2002] that Euclidean transformations of image space (spatio-intensity space) are inappropriate for image analysis.

A further conclusion is that the $L_2$-distance is inappropriate to measuring distances in these non-negative spaces. Still, many applications within image analysis and machine learning are based on the $L_2$-distance. More suitable alternatives, based on probabilistic modeling, are discussed in Chapter 6.

## 2.5    LINKS TO BIOLOGICALLY INSPIRED MODELS

As mentioned in the previous sections, channel representations originate mainly from technical requirements and principles, but were also inspired by biology [Granlund, 1999]. They share many similarities with population codes in computational neuroscience [Lüdtke et al., 2002, Pouget et al., 2003], which are conversely mainly motivated by observations in biological systems.

To complete confusion, the concept of population codes developed historically from approaches that used the term "channel codes" [Snippe and Koenderink, 1992]. Channel (or population) codes have been suggested repeatedly as a computational model for observations in human perception and cognition.

The term "channel" has also been used by Howard and Rogers [1995], writing about *sensory channels* that establish *labeled-line detectors*, which have a *bandpass tuning function*. The activation of these detectors happens through bell-shaped sensitivity curves and controls the frequency of firing.

The observation of firing rates in biological systems also inspired the approach of asynchronous networks based on spikes, the spikenets, proposed by Thorpe [2002]. The simple mechanisms, and in particular the non-negative nature of frequency, enables high-speed computations on low-resource systems.

However, activation-level-based, synchronous networks are more suitable for digital computers, including modern GPU-based systems, and thus most computational models for population codes. Intensity-based systems need different mechanisms than those based on sequences of spikes, but require regularization and enforcement of non-negativity.

The regularization of the number of active coefficients (or their $L_1$-norm) leads to the concept of sparse coding [Olshausen and Field, 1997]. Such systems are naturally robust and require few computations. Another regularization option is by means of continuity, resulting in the predictive coding paradigm [Rao and Ballard, 1999]. Also, this approach helps to design robust systems with low computational demand.

A further concern in coding systems is the design of an unbiased readout, i.e., no value-dependent systematic error occurs in the decoding [Denève et al., 2001]. The proposed iterative algorithm for the readout of population codes [Denève et al., 1999] is very similar to the newly published routing algorithm in deep networks [Sabour et al., 2017], but, as we will show in Chapter 5, not really unbiased.

Besides individual coding aspects, structural and topological knowledge from biological observation also are exploited in the design of systems, see e.g., the work by Riesenhuber and Poggio [1999]. Most of these works are to some extent based on the pioneering work of Hubel and Wiesel [1959]. Channel representations are no exception here as can be observed in Figure 2.4. The right-hand illustration has been generated with the channel representation and shares many similarities with the left part of the figure.

## SUMMARY

In this chapter we have given a short overview of statistical design principles for visual features, invariance/equivariance properties, sparse and compact representations, histograms, and signatures. We have provided a brief survey of the most important grid-based feature representations that are relevant to channel representations and CCFMs. Finally, we have related the channel representation to a number of approaches mainly inspired from biology. In the subsequent chapter we will now focus on the technical details of channel encoding, reflecting also on the relations to other feature extraction methods in more detail.

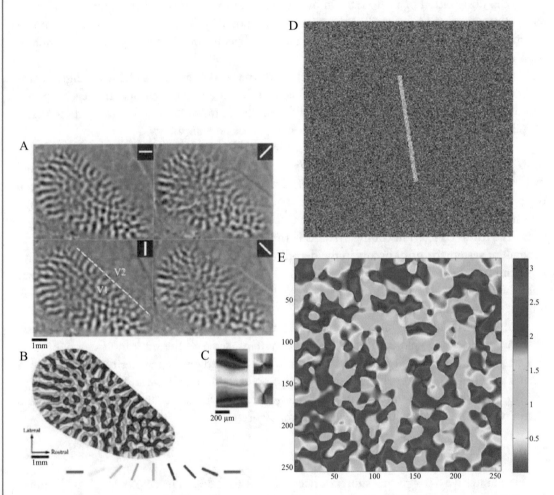

Figure 2.4: Left: reproduced with permission from Bosking et al. [1997]. A: parts of visual cortex active under orientation stimuli. B: orientation map obtained by vector summation. Right: figure from Felsberg et al. [2015]. D: stimulus. E: response from channel smoothing of orientation.

# CHAPTER 3

# Channel Coding of Features

As introduced in the previous chapter, *channel coding* is an efficient way to represent features in a grid-based approach. This chapter will formally define methods for channel coding, first in one (feature) dimension, then in several dimensions. These definitions will be used to define CCFMs and relate them to popular specific feature representations such as SIFT, HOG, and SHOT in Chapter 4.

## 3.1 CHANNEL CODING

This introduction to channel coding makes use of notation and derivations according to Jonsson and Felsberg [2005]. The channel representation is built by channel encoding samples $x^{(m)}$ from a distribution with density $p$, i.e., $x^{(m)} \sim p$, where $m \in \{1, \ldots, M\}$ is the sample index. For simplicity, we assume a random variable here, but later we will usually consider stochastic processes, i.e., $x^{(m)}$ becomes a function of spatial coordinates and channel coding is performed point-wise at each spatial location.

The channel endcoding of $x^{(m)}$ results in the *channel vector*

$$\mathbf{c}^{(m)} = \begin{bmatrix} c_1^{(m)} \\ \vdots \\ c_N^{(m)} \end{bmatrix} = \begin{bmatrix} K(x^{(m)} - \xi_1) \\ \vdots \\ K(x^{(m)} - \xi_N) \end{bmatrix}, \tag{3.1}$$

where $c_n \in \{1, \ldots, N\}$ denote the *channel coefficients*, $K()$ the encoding kernel, and $\xi_n$ the *channel centers*.

The simplest case of channel encoding is a histogram binning over gray scale values $x^{(m)} \in \{0, \ldots, 255\}$, which is obtained by choosing $N = 256$, $\xi_n = n - 1$ for all $n \in \{1, \ldots, 256\}$, and the rectangular kernel

$$K_R(x) = \begin{cases} 1 & |x| < 1/2 \\ 1/2 & |x| = 1/2 \\ 0 & \text{otherwise} \end{cases}. \tag{3.2}$$

It might appear trivial to explain histogram calculation as an example of channel coding, but this example is very useful to understand the general case later.

After binning (3.1), the normalized histogram is obtained by averaging over the sample set $\{x^{(m)}\}$ of size $M$. For stochastic processes, this sample set will often be formed by a local neighborhood [Felsberg et al., 2006] and averaging happens over the observed realization of the process, i.e., we assume weak ergodicity.

The $n$th histogram bin, or channel coefficient, becomes

$$c_n = \frac{1}{M} \sum_{m=1}^{M} c_n^{(m)} = \frac{1}{M} \sum_{m=1}^{M} K_R \left( x^{(m)} - n + 1 \right) . \tag{3.3}$$

Obviously, histograms over ranges of gray scales can easily be constructed by modifying the number of channels (or bins), $N$, and the channel (bin) centers $\xi_n$. In order to keep indices as integers, we will use the convention throughout this text that the domain of the samples is determined by the number of channels: $x^{(m)} \in [0; N) \subset \mathbb{R}$ (for histograms on discrete values, e.g., gray scale histogram, also $x^{(m)} \in \mathbb{Q}$).[1]

If the original integer samples are given in the range $\tilde{x}^{(m)} \in \{x_{\min}, \ldots, x_{\max}\}$, we apply the appropriate affine interval transformation:

$$x^{(m)} = \frac{N}{x_{\max} - x_{\min} + 1} \left( \tilde{x}^{(m)} - x_{\min} \right) . \tag{3.4}$$

For instance, if 256 gray scale values are supposed to be binned into $N = 8$ bins, i.e., 32 values are, respectively, mapped to one bin, we apply first (3.4), i.e., rescale all values by $1/32$, and $x^{(m)} \in [0; 8)$ (see Figure 2.3 for the case of $N = 7$).

If the original samples are from the continuous domain in the interval $\tilde{x}^{(m)} \in [x_{\min}; x_{\max})$, we apply the corresponding affine transformation:

$$x^{(m)} = \frac{N}{x_{\max} - x_{\min}} \left( \tilde{x}^{(m)} - x_{\min} \right) . \tag{3.5}$$

For instance, if line orientation values $\tilde{x}^{(m)} \in [0; \pi)$ are to be binned into 8 bins, we obtain $x^{(m)} = \frac{8}{\pi} \tilde{x}^{(m)}$.

To avoid problems regarding the discontinuity in $K_R(x)$, the bin centers are placed such that the edges never end up on discrete values. This is achieved by using the offset

$$x_0 = \frac{1}{2} \left( 1 + \frac{N}{x_{\max} - x_{\min} + 1} \right) \tag{3.6}$$

instead of 1 in (3.3). For $N = 256$, the offset is 1. For continuous samples $\tilde{x}^{(m)} \in [x_{\min}; x_{\max})$, the offset is set to $\frac{1}{2}(1 + \epsilon)$, where $\epsilon > 0$ such that the supremum $\sup \tilde{x}^{(m)} \leq x_{\max} - \epsilon$. This guarantees that no values hit the left edge of the first bin or the right edge of the last bin.

Channel coding is not restricted to rectangular kernels, but many types of polynomial, exponential, or trigonometric kernels can be applied [Forssén, 2004]. For the purpose of this

---

[1]For the case $N = 256$ above, we obtain $x^{(m)} \in [0; 256) \subset \mathbb{N}$, which is equivalent to $x^{(m)} \in \{0, \ldots, 255\}$.

text, we will make use of two specific kernels, namely linear B-splines

$$K_B(x) = \begin{cases} 1 - |x| & |x| \leq 1 \\ 0 & \text{otherwise} \end{cases} \qquad (3.7)$$

and $\cos^2$-kernels

$$K_C(x) = \begin{cases} \frac{2}{3} \cos^2(\pi x/3) & |x| \leq 3/2 \\ 0 & \text{otherwise} \end{cases} . \qquad (3.8)$$

All three kernels are illustrated in Figure 3.1.

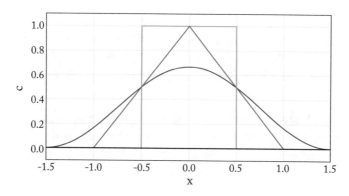

Figure 3.1: The three kernels used in this text: rectangular $K_R(x)$ (green), linear B-spline $K_B(x)$ (blue), and $\cos^2$-kernel $K_C(x)$ (red).

Compared to (3.3), only the offset of the channel centers and the relation between the number of channels $N$ and the size of the interval is modified for the different kernels:

$$c_n = \frac{1}{M} \sum_{m=1}^{M} K_B\left(x^{(m)} - n + 1\right) \qquad x^{(m)} \in [0; N - 1) \qquad (3.9)$$

$$c_n = \frac{1}{M} \sum_{m=1}^{M} K_C\left(x^{(m)} - n + 3/2\right) \qquad x^{(m)} \in [0; N - 2) . \qquad (3.10)$$

Thus, the offset $x_0$ for the linear B-spline kernel $K_B(x)$ is one and for the $\cos^2$-kernel $K_C(x)$ it is 3/2. More in general, the wider the kernel, the larger the offset. Note that the formulation above is chosen such that the overlap between kernels is minimized under the constraint that the sum over $n$ is constant. Other choices have been investigated by Forssén [2004], leading, however, to increased redundancy of the representation.

The relative placement of the kernelized bins for all three cases are illustrated in Figure 3.2, where the number of channels $N$ has been increased by one and two for the B-spline kernel and the $\cos^2$-kernel, respectively.

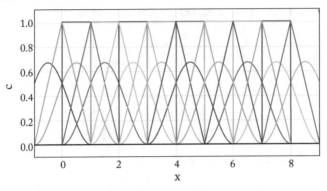

Figure 3.2: Kernelized histograms over the interval $[0; 8)$ for the three kernels used in this text: rectangular $K_R(x)$ (8 bins), linear B-spline $K_B(x)$ (9 bins), and $\cos^2$-kernel $K_C(x)$ (10 bins). The number of bins has been adapted in order to have the same density of bins.

The extra channels are required due to the overlap of the kernels, since each value within the coding interval needs to be represented by the same number of active kernels and the kernels at the boundary have no outer neighbors to overlap with. For periodic domains, this observation obviously does not apply and no extra channels are required:

$$x^{(m)} \in [0; N - \Delta N), \tag{3.11}$$

where

$$\Delta N = \begin{cases} 2 & \text{if non-periodic domain and } K_C \\ 1 & \text{if non-periodic domain and } K_B \\ 0 & \text{if periodic domain or } K_R \end{cases} \tag{3.12}$$

and (3.5) becomes in general

$$x^{(m)} = \frac{N - \Delta N}{x_{\max} - x_{\min}} \left( \tilde{x}^{(m)} - x_{\min} \right) . \tag{3.13}$$

For continuous samples, we can therefore write

$$x_0 = \frac{\Delta N + 1}{2}, \tag{3.14}$$

but often we do not explicitly mention the offset if it is not relevant.

One well-known result from the literature is that histograms result in an approximation of the sample density $p$, filtered by the applied kernel [Bishop, 1995]. Thus, the expectation of $c_n$ is

$$E[c_n] = \int_{-\infty}^{\infty} p(x) K(x - \xi_n) \, dx , \tag{3.15}$$

and the channel coefficients are linear features of the density that we are interested in. This property will be used in the next chapter for decoding channel representations.

Another consequence of the choice of kernels and their placement is that

$$\sum_{n=1}^{N} c_n = 1 \qquad \text{if all } x^{(m)} \in [0; N - \Delta N) \ . \tag{3.16}$$

The proof is easy and left to the reader. Another property that is easy to show is that $\cos^2$-kernels also have a constant sum of squares independent of $x$ [Nordberg et al., 1994]:

$$\sum_{n=1}^{N} K_{\mathrm{C}}^2 \left( x^{(m)} - n + 3/2 \right) = 1/2 \qquad \text{for all } x^{(m)} \in [0; N - \Delta N) \ . \tag{3.17}$$

Note that this property does not hold for linear B-splines or any other continuous positive-definite kernel [Felsberg et al., 2015], but obviously it holds for the rectangular kernel at nearly all $x$.

So far, we have only encoded one-dimensional samples $x$, but before we consider multi-dimensional encodings, we will focus on one application: visual object tracking.

## 3.2 ENHANCED DISTRIBUTION FIELD TRACKING

Local averaging of channel representations within a bounding box has been used successfully in object tracking [Danelljan et al., 2015, Felsberg, 2013, Sevilla-Lara and Learned-Miller, 2012], i.e., for video analysis. Visual object tracking is defined as the causal, model-free sequential detection of a single object in an image sequence [Kristan, Leonardis, Matas, Felsberg, Pflugfelder and et al., 2016]. The only available information about the object to be tracked is its bounding-box in the first frame; this is why it is called generic or model-free. The tracking method may build an internal model based on the bounding-box contents in the first frame and may also update its internal model on the fly, but only information from previous and the current frame may be used (causality).

Enhanced distribution field tracking (EDFT, Felsberg [2013]) builds on distribution field tracking (DFT) by Sevilla-Lara and Learned-Miller [2012], a visual object tracking method that is based on comparing smoothed local histograms of the image patch inside the bounding-box. The original DFT algorithm was developed independently of the concept of channel representations and differs in mainly one property, namely that the bins are smoothed after the accumulation.

The image intensity (gray scale) $I(i, j)$ is considered a stochastic variable and its distribution is estimated by spatially weighted histograms using $K_{\mathrm{R}}(x)$ and $N = 16$, i.e., $x^{(i,j)} = \frac{I(i,j)}{16}$ (see (3.4)):

$$c_n = \sum_{i,j} w_{(i,j)} c_n^{(i,j)} = \sum_{i,j} w_{(i,j)} K_{\mathrm{R}} \left( x^{(i,j)} - n + 17/32 \right) \ , \tag{3.18}$$

where the offset has been computed according to (3.6) and $w_{(i,j)}$ denotes the spatial weights, a 2D Gaussian kernel $h_\sigma(i, j)$ with standard deviation $\sigma$.

The original DFT approach is a multi-scale algorithm typically using three different standard deviations, but for simplifying the subsequent arguments, we ignore this detail and stick to the single-scale case.

The next step of DFT after accumulating histogram values locally is to smooth the coefficients $c_n$ along the channel index $n$ using a 1D Gaussian kernel and results in the DF $d(i, j, n)$. This is the post-smoothing step previously mentioned.

During the tracking, the DF of the internal model, $d_{\text{model}}$, is compared to the DF of a bounding-box in the current frame, $d_f$, within a local search window. The distance measure used is the sum of absolute differences, i.e.,

$$L_1(d_{\text{model}}, d_f) = \sum_{i,j,n} |d_{\text{model}}(i, j, n) - d_f(i, j, n)| \ . \tag{3.19}$$

The displacement is estimated by local search of the minimum $L_1$ error within a window of maximum displacement, a further parameter of the method chosen as 30 pixels according to Sevilla-Lara and Learned-Miller [2012].

When the best-fitting position has been found, the current template $d_{\text{model},t}$ is updated with the current DF $d_f$ using linear weights $\lambda = 0.95$ for the previous template and $(1 - \lambda) = 0.05$ for the novel patch

$$d_{\text{model},t+1}(i, j, n) = \lambda d_{\text{model},t}(i, j, n) + (1 - \lambda)d_f(i, j, ci). \tag{3.20}$$

Due to the density-based comparison, the method is robust against outliers, and due to the template-update, the method can also deal with continuous changes of object aspects and the lighting [Sevilla-Lara and Learned-Miller, 2012].

EDFT enhances DFT in various ways [Felsberg, 2013], but most importantly, the post-smoothing of histograms (rectangular kernels) is replaced with a quadratic B-spline channel representation, i.e., pre-smoothing before binning, and results in significant improvements. In later versions of EDFT, $\cos^2$-kernels have been used instead, giving further improvements [Öfjäll and Felsberg, 2014b], also based on a modified model update (3.20) and distance measure (3.19).

The model update in (3.20) has been replaced with a power-update rule

$$c_{\text{model},t+1,n}^{(i,j)} = \left(\lambda \left(c_{\text{model},t,n}^{(i,j)}\right)^q + (1 - \lambda)\left(c_{f,n}^{(i,j)}\right)^q\right)^{1/q} \tag{3.21}$$

and a coherence weight has been introduced to the distance measure (3.19)

$$L_1^w(\mathbf{c}_{\text{model}}, \mathbf{c}_f) = \sum_{i,j,n} \text{coh}(\mathbf{c}^{i,j}) \left|c_{\text{model},n}^{(i,j)} - c_{f,n}^{(i,j)}\right| \ . \tag{3.22}$$

The coherence measure will be formally introduced in Chapter 5, but it can easily be explained using Figure 3.3. Coherent regions imply that the information in the distribution is highly discriminative. Incoherent regions imply that the distribution is uninformative. The discriminative power can be further increased by incorporating orientation and color information, but this will require multi-dimensional coding.

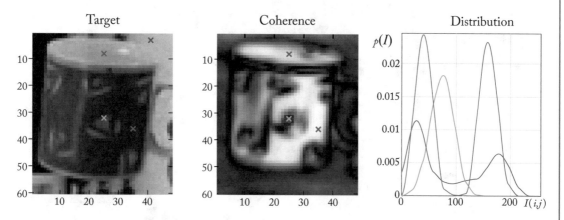

Figure 3.3: Target and target model representation at the end of the VOT2013 cup-sequence. Left: found target patch. Middle: coherence of the target model (black: low, white: high). Right: represented pixel value distributions for a selection of points marked in left and middle images. Large coherence correspond to static pixel values on the tracked object (blue, magenta, highly peaked distribution). Low coherence corresponds to background pixels (red, multi-modal distribution) and varying pixels on the target (green, wide distribution). Figure from Öfjäll and Felsberg [2014b].

The local averaging of channel representations can also be used to increase the discriminative power of spatial mixture models and thus for methods that apply those models for detection, recognition, or registration. For colored point cloud registration, Danelljan et al. [2016] have combined channel representations of color with spatial GMMs, see Figure 3.4.

## 3.3 ORIENTATION SCORES AS CHANNEL REPRESENTATIONS

In this section, we consider the specific case of channel-coded local orientation over the spatial domain, i.e., the channel-coded feature is the local orientation. In the 2D case, this corresponds to the angle $\theta$ at all positions $(i, j)$ encoded in channels, resulting in a 3D array, see Figure 3.5. According to Duits, Felsberg, Granlund and ter Haar Romeny [2007], this approach is closely related to orientation scores as introduced by Duits, Duits, van Almsick and ter Haar Romeny [2007], with its main concepts presented in Figure 3.5.

Orientation scores are closely related to wavelets. In a nutshell, whereas wavelets are based on the group consisting of scaling and translation [Mallat, 1989], orientation scores are based on the Euclidean group (translation and rotation). This change of group setting also implies that

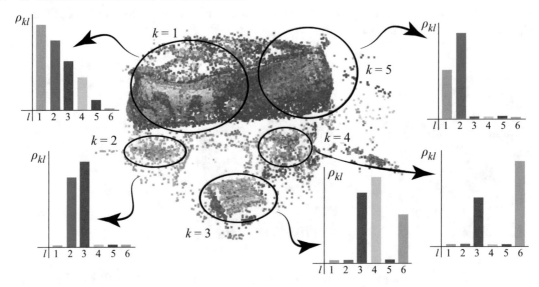

Figure 3.4: Combining color distribution estimates for five different spatial regions (indexed by $k$). Each spatial distribution has its own color histogram. The combined distributions are then used for point set registration. Illustration by Danelljan et al. [2016] used with permission.

the wavelet approach needs to be generalized[2] to meet the requirements of orientation scores. In particular, the reconstruction from orientation scores is based on the theory of reproducing kernel Hilbert spaces.

As a motivating example, consider the four kernels in Figure 3.6 (adapted example from Duits, Duits, van Almsick and ter Haar Romeny [2007]): convolving an image with all four kernels and adding the four resulting images will result in the original image.

The result from these four convolutions may be considered as a representation with 4 channels and the decoding is achieved by simply summing the channel coefficients for each spatial position.

The most general formulation of orientation scores assumes continuous parameters of the Euclidean motion, but the relation to channel coding is implying a restriction to discrete orientations. Thus, we consider the group[3] $G = \mathbb{T}_N \rtimes \mathbb{R}^2$, $\mathbb{T}_N = \{2\pi n/N \,|\, n = 0, \ldots, N-1\}$ and get [Duits, Felsberg, Granlund and ter Haar Romeny, 2007]

$$U_x^N(i, j, n) = (\mathcal{R}_{2\pi n/N} \psi * x)(i, j) \ , \tag{3.23}$$

---

[2]For the interested reader: the required representation is reducible whereas wavelet theory requires irreducible representations as shown by Duits, Duits, van Almsick and ter Haar Romeny [2007].

[3]In the original work by Duits, Duits, van Almsick and ter Haar Romeny [2007], rotations are represented by complex exponentials of the angle, but here we chose to denote the angles for the sake of shorter formulations.

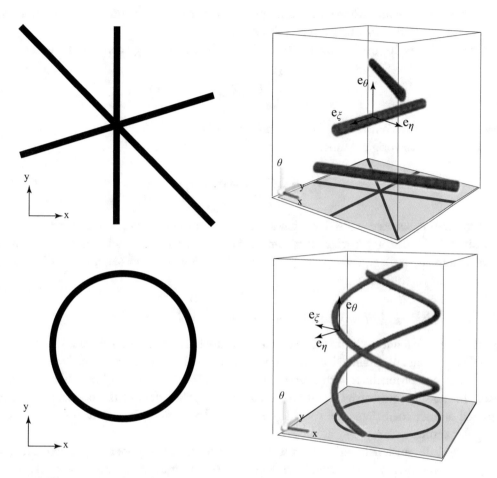

Figure 3.5: Illustration of orientation scores for an image containing three bars (top) and a circle (bottom). Figure courtesy Bekkers et al. [2014]. Note that in the text, we use $(i, j)$ instead of $(x, y)$.

$$
\begin{array}{|c|c|c|}
\hline
0 & -\frac{1}{12} & 0 \\
\hline
-\frac{1}{12} & \frac{1}{4} & \frac{1}{4} \\
\hline
0 & -\frac{1}{12} & 0 \\
\hline
\end{array}
+
\begin{array}{|c|c|c|}
\hline
0 & \frac{1}{4} & 0 \\
\hline
-\frac{1}{12} & \frac{1}{4} & -\frac{1}{12} \\
\hline
0 & -\frac{1}{12} & 0 \\
\hline
\end{array}
+
\begin{array}{|c|c|c|}
\hline
0 & -\frac{1}{12} & 0 \\
\hline
\frac{1}{4} & \frac{1}{4} & -\frac{1}{12} \\
\hline
0 & -\frac{1}{12} & 0 \\
\hline
\end{array}
+
\begin{array}{|c|c|c|}
\hline
0 & -\frac{1}{12} & 0 \\
\hline
-\frac{1}{12} & \frac{1}{4} & -\frac{1}{12} \\
\hline
0 & \frac{1}{4} & 0 \\
\hline
\end{array}
=
\begin{array}{|c|c|c|}
\hline
0 & 0 & 0 \\
\hline
0 & 1 & 0 \\
\hline
0 & 0 & 0 \\
\hline
\end{array}
$$

Figure 3.6: Adapted example from Duits, Duits, van Almsick and ter Haar Romeny [2007]. The sum of the four kernels results in the identity operator, such that the sum of the four filtering outputs is equal to the input.

where $*$ denotes the convolution (thus scalar products over all translations), $\mathcal{R}_\alpha$ a rotation by $\alpha$, and $\psi$ the kernel of the orientation score, the wavelet.

In order to enable well-posed reconstruction, $\psi$ must fulfill an energy constraint based on

$$M_\psi(u, v) = \frac{1}{N} \sum_{n=0}^{N-1} |\mathcal{F}(\mathcal{R}_{2\pi n/N} \psi)(u, v)|^2 \ , \tag{3.24}$$

where $\mathcal{F}$ denotes the Fourier transform from $(i, j)$ to $(u, v)$.

If $M_\psi = 1$, the original function $x$ can by reconstructed as

$$\tilde{x}(i, j) = \sum_{n=0}^{N-1} U_x^N(i, j, n) \ . \tag{3.25}$$

Orientation scores can also be extended to the similitude group, as suggested by Sharma and Duits [2015]. The approach is very similar to calculating a channel representation in the log-polar domain, see e.g., Öfjäll and Felsberg [2017]. For this approach, multi-dimensional channel coding is required.

## 3.4   MULTI-DIMENSIONAL CODING

In previous sections, only one-dimensional random variables $x$ have been considered. The channel coefficients that are obtained by coding one-dimensional variables are basically stochastically independent, except for those with overlapping kernels, i.e., the two neighbors in case of $\cos^2$-kernels. In the subsequent considerations in this section, the effect of the overlapping kernels is ignored and all coefficients are considered independent, which is strictly true only for the rectangular kernel.

If multi-dimensional random vectors with independent components are encoded, all dimensions can be encoded and stored independently. After summing over all observed samples, the densities of the marginal distributions are obtained and since those are independent, an estimate of the joint estimate is obtained by multiplying these marginal estimates. For two-dimensional samples $(x_1, x_2)$ with channel coefficients $(c_{1,n_1}, c_{2,n_2})$, we obtain by (3.15)

$$\begin{aligned} \mathrm{E}[c_{1,n_1}]\mathrm{E}[c_{2,n_2}] \ &= \ \int p(x_1)K(x_1 - \xi_{1,n_1})\, dx_1 \int p(x_2)K(x_2 - \xi_{2,n_2})\, dx_2 & (3.26) \\ &= \ \iint p(x_1, x_2)K(x_1 - \xi_{1,n_1})K(x_2 - \xi_{2,n_2})\, dx_1 dx_2 & (3.27) \\ &= \ \mathrm{E}[c_{1,n_1}c_{2,n_2}] \ . & (3.28) \end{aligned}$$

One such case is color and orientation in a local region, see Figure 3.7.

In general, one might assume that color and orientation are mutually independent and the joint distribution can be computed by multiplying the marginal distributions of color and orientation.

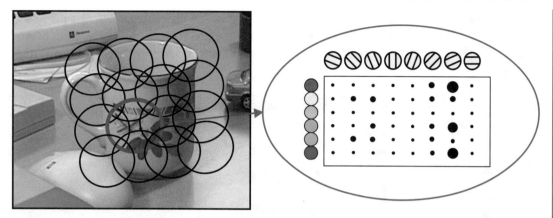

Figure 3.7: Simultaneous encoding of color and orientation in a local image region. Figure taken from Jonsson [2008] courtesy Erik Jonsson. The red circle on the left indicates the considered local region and the color and orientation patterns on the right represent the channels of the marginal distributions. In the present example, color and orientation are not completely independent, such that the channel matrix, represented by the black blobs, cannot be factorized.

If the components of the random vector are not mutually independent, for instance because the observed objects, such as bananas or skyscrapers, lead to color-dependent orientation distributions, the identity leading to (3.27) breaks. This effect has also been observed in the case of texture classification by Khan et al. [2013].

In the general case, the expectation of the product of channel coefficients can thus not be computed from the product of their expectations,

$$\mathrm{E}[c_{1,n_1}]\mathrm{E}[c_{2,n_2}] \neq \mathrm{E}[c_{1,n_1}c_{2,n_2}] \ , \qquad (3.29)$$

implying that summation over the sample index must happen after the outer product of channel vectors.

One such example are optical flow vectors, where moving edges and lines have highly correlated spatial displacements [Spies and Forssén, 2003]. Obviously, this leads to an exponential growth of the number of coefficients with the number of dimensions. If all $d$ dimensions are encoded with the same number of channels $N$, the total number of coefficients becomes $N^d$.

In practice, however, this is seldom a problem. In many cases, not all product terms stemming from the outer products are required, e.g., Granlund [2000b] suggests to only use second order terms, or the mutual dependency can be ignored altogether without compromising the results [Wallenberg et al., 2011].

In the latter work, RGB color and depth gradients ($\Delta$D), which both have a two-dimensional correlation structure, are channel coded and concatenated. This approach leads to improved segmentation performance, see Figure 3.8. Presumably, the segmentation performance could be further improved by replacing RGB values with color names, the previously mentioned 11-dimensional learned soft-assignment suggested by Van De Weijer et al. [2009] that shares also similarities to channel representations, but this pathway has not been further explored.

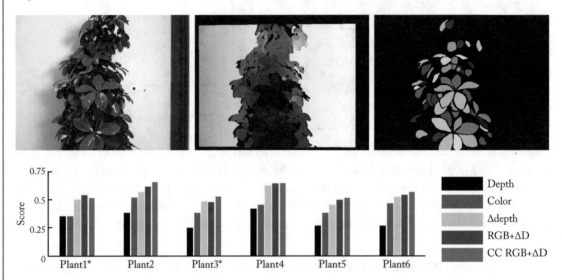

Figure 3.8: Top from left to right: plant 5 from the plant data set (Wallenberg et al. [2011]) RGB, depth, and ground truth segmentation. Bottom: consensus scores by various feature combinations. Images indicated with asterisks were used for parameter tuning of all compared methods. Note that although RGB+$\Delta$D and channel-coded RGB+$\Delta$D have similar results on the tuning images, channel-coded RGB+$\Delta$D has a higher score on all evaluation images.

Even if all possible combinations of channel coefficients are taken into account, the total number of non-zero products has an upper bound which is linear in the number of observed samples as observed by Felsberg and Granlund [2006].

In that work, three performance experiments have been conducted where a number $M$ of samples in spaces of dimension $d = 1 \dots 9$ have been encoded with $N$ channels in each dimension, see Figure 3.9. The comparison of time consumption for $M = 5,000$ and $M = 10,000$ samples and $N = 10$ shows a proportional increase with the number of samples. The comparison of $N = 10$ and $N = 20$ for $M = 10,000$ samples shows no increase of time consumption. Thus, if sparse data structures are used to store the coefficient matrices, a brute-force outer product of all dimensions is feasible and still allows for real-time performance [Felsberg and Hedborg, 2007b, Pagani et al., 2009].

Interestingly, the absence of observations for most of the products gets completely different meanings in a frequentist and a bayesian interpretation: The former simply assumes zero probability, whereas the latter computes a non-zero probability depending on the assumed prior

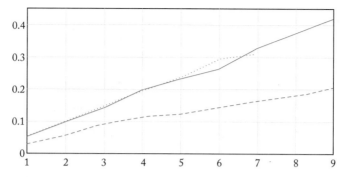

Figure 3.9: Time consumption for encoding, implemented in Matlab on a Powerbook with 1 GHz PPC. Ordinate: dimensions $d = 1 \ldots 9$, abscissa: time in seconds (averaged over 10 runs). Dashed line: 5,000 samples, $10^d$ channels. Solid line: 10,000 samples, $10^d$ channels. Dotted line: 10,000 samples, $20^d$ channels. Figure from Felsberg and Hedborg [2007b].

(e.g., a Dirichlet distribution, see also Chapter 6) and the total number of observations falling into other bins. However, in either case, the estimate for the density can be computed from the sparse data structure.

With the introduction of P-channels [Felsberg and Granlund, 2006] a computationally more efficient approximation to compute linear B-spline kernels has been introduced. Besides the computational considerations, also *explicit spatial pooling* has been suggested.

Instead of computing local averages over image regions and maintaining the image resolution, as e.g., suggested by Felsberg and Granlund [2003], the channel representations are simultaneously low-pass filtered and down-sampled, reducing the computational effort further. This spatial pooling is *explicit*, because the local coordinates are also considered as part of the random vector. The vector now contains a part with spatial coordinates and a feature part, together forming the *spatio-featural space* proposed by Jonsson and Felsberg [2009]. This approach will be further considered in the subsequent chapter.

## SUMMARY

In this chapter we have introduced the channel encoding of visual features. The resulting representation is an efficient approximation of a kernel density estimator for the distribution of the encoded features. We have related the approach to population coding, DFs, and orientation scores. In the subsequent chapter we will now focus on spatial maps of channel encoded features, i.e., CCFMs and their relation to popular 2D features such as SIFT and HOG and 3D features such as SHOT.

C H A P T E R   4

# Channel-Coded Feature Maps

As introduced in the second chapter, *channel-coded feature maps* (CCFMs) establish a specific family of grid-based feature representations. This chapter will extend the methods for channel coding of features to spatial dimensions and thus introduce CCFMs. Using its formal definition, popular specific feature representations such as SIFT and HOG (2D) and SHOT (3D) will be expressed in terms of CCFMs.

## 4.1   DEFINITION OF CHANNEL-CODED FEATURE MAPS

Channel representations on the spatio-featural space (SF-space) have been introduced as CCFMs by Jonsson [2008]. Intuitively, CCFMs simply combine channel vectors for a grid of local areas; see Figure 3.7, left. All theory is decribed for a two-dimensional spatial domain $\Omega$ with indices $(i, j)$ below, but obviously the theory generalizes to 3D and spatio-temporal domains as well.

Assume that $d$ features $x_3(i, j), \ldots, x_{d+2}(i, j)$ are given for all spatial positions $(i, j) \in \Omega$. Define the additional two spatial features ($N_{1,2}$ are the numbers of channels in $i, j$ and $\Delta N$ is defined in (3.12)):

$$x_1(i, j) = \frac{N_1 - \Delta N}{i_{\max} - i_{\min}}(i - i_{\min}) \qquad x_2(i, j) = \frac{N_2 - \Delta N}{j_{\max} - j_{\min}}(j - j_{\min}) \ . \tag{4.1}$$

The corresponding $(d + 2)$-dimensional SF-space is then formed as

$$\mathrm{SF}(x_3, \ldots, x_{d+2}) = \{(x_1(i, j), \ldots, x_{d+2}(i, j))\}_{(i,j)\in\Omega} \ , \tag{4.2}$$

i.e., the set of $d$ 2D functions has been turned into a list of $|\Omega|$ $(d + 2)$-D vectors. The CCFM is then obtained by channel coding the vectors in this list and summing over all elements. The coding is done in an outer product way, i.e.,

$$\mathrm{CCFM}(n_1, \ldots, n_{d+2}) = \sum_{(i,j)\in\Omega} \prod_{l=1}^{d+2} K(x_l(i, j) - \xi_{l,n_l}) \ . \tag{4.3}$$

CCFMs can be used as input for supervised learning of various vision problems such as object recognition, detection, and pose estimation [Johansson et al., 2006, Jonsson, 2008, Jonsson and Felsberg, 2009] (see Figure 4.1), and are closely related to HOG and SIFT features; see the Sections 4.2 and 4.3.

Figure 4.1: Two example frames illustrating simultaneous detection and pose estimation using CCFMs. The detection is performed by matching CCFMs of prototype poses, recorded on a 3D rotation table, with CCFMs in the current frame, see Section 4.2. The pose is illustrated by an edge image of the matched prototype. Figure based on Jonsson [2008].

They can also be used in weakly supervised online learning of correspondence between views [Felsberg et al., 2013], a method that uses divergences to define the distance measure between distributions instead of the $L_2$-distance; see Chapter 6. All previously mentioned machine learning approaches can be used to address the problem of situation awareness with the purpose of robot control.

As an alternative, robot vision can also be approached as a *robust regression learning* problem, directly mapping from visual input CCFMs to channel representations of motor control. As a learning mechanism, Öfjäll and Felsberg [2014a] have applied a simple Hebbian learning rule. Interestingly, the typical problems of Hebbian learning, e.g., regarding stability, are avoided due to the boundedness of channel representations. As quantitative results are difficult to compare on an online learning robotic system, quantitative comparisons with robust regression [Huang et al., 2012] and *random forest regression* Liaw and Wiener [2002] have been made on the Multi-PIE dataset Gross et al. [2010]; see Figure 4.2.

In order to speed-up their calculation, (4.3) can either be broken down to monopieces [Jonsson and Felsberg, 2009], i.e., the SF-space is projected onto a small set of basis elements and the resulting coefficients are then used to compute the CCFM components, or the computation can be done incrementally.

In this approach proposed by Felsberg [2010], a *spatio-featural scale-space* (SF-scale-space) is constructed and the CCFM is computed in a pyramid approach. While the spatial resolution is decimated in each step, the feature resolution is simultaneously increased. Thus, SSFMs with low spatial resolution have a high feature resolution and vice versa; see Figure 4.3.

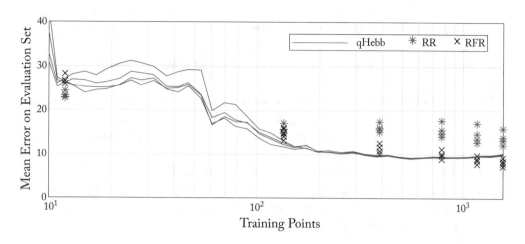

Figure 4.2: Hebbian learning on channel-coded visual features is superior to robust regression and random forest regression for the pose estimation task on the Multi-PIE dataset. Plot by Öfjäll and Felsberg [2014a].

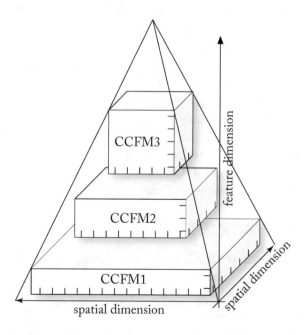

Figure 4.3: Going upward in the SF-pyramid reduces spatial resolution and increases feature resolution. Going downward reduces feature resolution and increases spatial resolution. Figure based on Felsberg [2010].

Note that both approaches have been formulated for B-spline basis functions, resulting in linear operators for down-sampling. For $\cos^2$-kernels, that approach cannot be applied directly.

In this context, a similar question arises as for the tensor resolutions in deep networks: How to choose the spatial pooling, the number of feature channels, and how are these two parameters connected?

For CCFMs this question has been addressed by an approach inspired by the *isotropic model* [Koenderink and van Doorn, 2002]. In this model, no out-of-plane rotations in image space are allowed, as these would mix densities and spatial coordinates. Instead, shearing transformations are applied to the image space.

Applying this approach to SF-space instead results in an SF-uncertainty relation, as formulated by Felsberg [2009]. Similar to the lower bound on the product of position and impulse uncertainties in Heisenberg's uncertainty relation, a lower bound for the product of spatial resolution and feature resolution has been derived:

$$(\Delta i)(\Delta x) \geq \frac{1}{2}\sigma_i \sigma_x, \tag{4.4}$$

where $\sigma_x^2$ is the intrinsic variance of the feature domain, e.g., for intensities given by the quantization noise, and $\sigma_i^2$ is the intrinsic variance of the spatial domain, e.g., given by the discretization (sampling distance). Note that compared to the original work [Felsberg, 2009] the notation has changed ($f$ became $x$ and $x$ became $i$).

Using this lower bound, a particular choice for the spatial resolution implies a maximum number of feature channels and a certain choice of feature channels implies a maximum spatial resolution. The respective maximum has to be seen in the sense that higher resolutions will not lead to increased information content, only to increased redundancy. These bounds have been used for the incremental CCFM calculation [Felsberg, 2010]; see Figure 4.4.

Presumably, these bounds are also relevant for the choice of parameters in deep networks and other feature descriptors such as HOG and SIFT. The connection to the latter two approaches is derived in the subsequent two sections.

## 4.2  THE HOG DESCRIPTOR AS A CCFM

Popular feature descriptors such as HOG, [Dalal and Triggs, 2005] and the descriptor in the SIFT, [Lowe, 2004] are based on local orientation information extracted from the image during pre-processing. As pointed out by Dalal and Triggs [2005] and already earlier investigated by [Johansson, 2004, p. 35], it is preferable to estimate local orientation with the smallest possible filters and to compensate for the noise in later steps when building the descriptor in a non-linear way.

In the HOG descriptor, centralized differences are used to estimate the gradient $\nabla I(i, j)$. The gradient orientation $\theta(i, j) = \arg(\nabla I(i, j)) \in [0; \pi)$ is then binned into a 9-bin histogram over a local cell, weighted by the respective magnitude $|\nabla I(i, j)|$. Note that the HOG descriptor

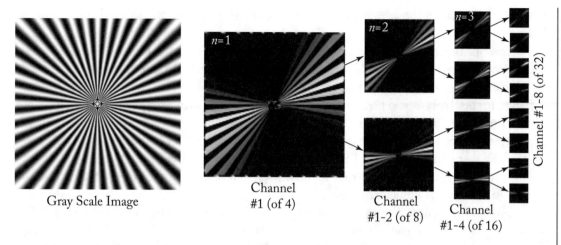

Gray Scale Image

Channel #1 (of 4)

Channel #1-2 (of 8)

Channel #1-4 (of 16)

Channel #1-8 (of 32)

Figure 4.4: Incrementally computed orientation pyramid. From left to right: image and hierarchy levels 1 ... 4. With each level, the orientation selectivity increases, while the spatial resolution decreases. Figure from Felsberg [2010].

does not use rectangular bins, but linear B-splines ("votes are interpolated bilinearly between the neighboring bin centers in both orientation and position;" Dalal and Triggs [2005]).

The number of orientation bins is chosen as $N = 9$. Note further that the orientation domain is periodic and we apply (3.13) to map the orientation to the interval $[-\frac{1}{2}; N - \frac{1}{2})$ ($\Delta N = 0$), because the last bin is identical to the first one, and the offset is arbitrary: $x_3(i, j) = \frac{9}{\pi}\theta(i, j) - \frac{1}{2}$.

We then compute a weighted version of (3.9), where the offset becomes irrelevant due to the periodicity of the domain and is chosen $x_0 = 1$ to simplify notation further down:

$$c_n = \sum_{(i,j)\in\text{cell}} |\nabla I(i, j)| K_B(x_3(i, j) - n + 1) \qquad n \in \{1, \ldots, 9\} \ . \tag{4.5}$$

As we will see further below, SIFT uses, differently from HOG, signed orientation information (direction). Dalal and Triggs [2005] argue that "for humans, [...] makes the signs of contrasts uninformative" whereas this is different for cars and motorbikes. Without diving into the debate of orientation vs. direction [Jähne, 2005, p. 342] and [Felsberg, 2002, p. 6], this is obviously a matter of invariance. Due to changes of illumination, contrast can be locally inverted and thus the local phase is inverted. For this case, (unsigned) orientations are mapped to the same bin, whereas directions are mapped to bins with opposing directional sense.

Simply ignoring the sign, i.e., the directional sense, is a case of weak invariance and for each single measurement some information, and thus discriminative power, is lost. If invariance is not required (cars, motorbikes), this results in degraded performance, whereas if invariance is required (humans), the advantage of weak invariance dominates the reduced discriminative power.

It would be interesting to repeat the comparison for 9 orientation bins vs. 18 direction bins using strong invariance. This could be achieved by duplicating the 18 bins histogram, shifting it by 9 bins, and then using the one that results in better performance, e.g., by using a latent binary variable. In total, this should give better discriminative power than using 9 orientation bins, but at the same level of invariance against contrast changes. Although this is a reasonable hypothesis, it remains to be shown in future experiments, e.g., defining EHOG (enhanced HOG).

A further parameter beyond the number of channels is the cell size. Whereas Dalal and Triggs [2005] suggest $6 \times 6$ cells, they are often referred to using $8 \times 8$ cells (which is also the default in the original implementation[1]).

For normalization, the cells are arranged in blocks. For rectangular blocks (R-HOG), Dalal and Triggs [2005] suggest using $3 \times 3$ cells, but are often referred to using $2 \times 2$ cells (also default in the implementation). Thus, each block basically corresponds to a CCFM, where the cells correspond to the spatial channels ($3 \times 3$, respectively, $2 \times 2$).

The kernel function used is again a linear B-spline. In contrast to the orientation domain, the spatial domain is not periodic and thus the channel centers have to be chosen appropriately on the edges of the cells. However, the original HOG implementation uses the same bin alignment for linearly interpolated histograms ("precision histograms" in the implementation) as for ordinary histograms and thus all orientation values that are close to the block borders have a lower impact on the descriptor. Whether this is a wanted effect remains unknown and Dalal and Triggs [2005] suggest a spatial Gaussian windowing $g(i, j)$ of the block anyway.

If we want to distinguish explicitly between a spatial weighting in the block and the computation of the interpolated histogram, the number of bins needs to be increased to $4 \times 4$ (respectively $3 \times 3$) and we compute the spatial features

$$x_1(i, j) = \frac{N-1}{i_{\max} - i_{\min}}(i - i_{\min}) \qquad x_2(i, j) = \frac{N-1}{j_{\max} - j_{\min}}(j - j_{\min}) \qquad (4.6)$$

with $N = 4$ (respectively, $N = 3$). The denominators are also determined by the product of cell size and cell numbers, i.e., $6 \cdot 3 = 18$, respectively, $8 \cdot 2 = 16$ pixels. The descriptor is then obtained by

$$\text{CCFM}(n_1, n_2, n_3) = \sum_{(i,j) \in \Omega} g(i, j) |\nabla I(i, j)| \prod_{l=1}^{3} K_{\mathrm{B}}(x_l(i, j) - n_l + 1) \qquad (4.7)$$

with indices $n_1, n_2 \in \{1, \ldots, 4(\text{or } 3)\}, n_3 \in \{1, \ldots, 9\}$. Note that in this definition, as pointed out above, the number of spatial bins is increased in each spatial dimension and the boundary bins are centered on the borders of the region.

---

[1]http://pascal.inrialpes.fr/soft/olt/learcode.zip

If (4.7) is supposed to give exactly the same numerical values as in the original HOG implementation, we need to apply some changes: $n_1, n_2 \in \{1, \ldots, 3(\text{or } 2)\}$, replace $N - 1$ with $N$ in (4.6), and $+1$ with $+1/2$ in (4.7); see Figure 4.5.

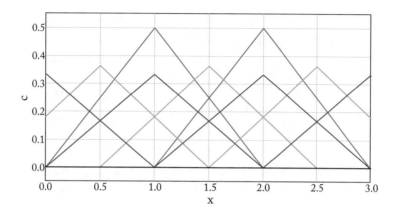

Figure 4.5: Relation between bins and spatial support in HOG (green), SIFT (blue), and CCFM (red).

The descriptor of the block is finally obtained by stacking all the coefficient into one vector and subsequent normalization. The dense descriptor over the full image (or image region) is then obtained by striding the block descriptor computation, *strided computation*, i.e., the descriptor is not computed for every pixel position, but only every ninth or eigth position (stride 9, respectively, 8). For $16 \times 16$ blocks, also stride 4 has been evaluated with good results [Dalal and Triggs, 2005].

In contrast to HOG, CCFMs have mostly been considered without spatial weighting in the block and with zero overlap, i.e., stride equal to the block size [Jonsson, 2008]. Results in object detection using this approach have been very promising [Jonsson and Felsberg, 2007], although only simple local matching has been used instead of discriminative, learned classifiers such as SVMs. On the other hand, also rotation and scale matching have been addressed; see Figure 4.6. Comparisons to HOG remain to be done in future work.

## 4.3    THE SIFT DESCRIPTOR AS A CCFM

In contrast to HOG, the SIFT descriptor has already been compared to CCFMs by Felsberg and Hedborg [2007a]. The kernels used in that work are a decomposition of linear kernels, called P-channels [Felsberg and Granlund, 2006], and in implementation very similar to the precision histograms from HOG [Dalal and Triggs, 2005]. The comparison also considers color extensions of the descriptors.

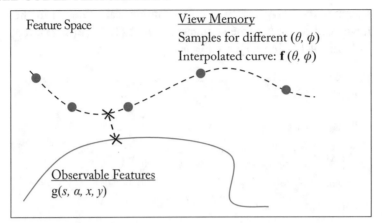

Figure 4.6: In the simultaneous view interpolation and tracking approach based on Jonsson [2008], matching is performed over scale, orientation, and position $(s, \alpha, x, y)$.

The SIFT descriptor by Lowe [2004] shares similarities with a HOG descriptor with block-size $16 \times 16$ and $4 \times 4$ cells, resulting in cell size $4 \times 4$. Instead of 9 orientation bins ($20°$ inter-bin distance), the SIFT descriptor uses 8 direction bins ($45°$ inter-bin distance).

A further difference is that the SIFT descriptor is computed at a previously detected scale and the direction measurements are made with respect to a previously determined reference direction.

Also, the "trilinear interpolation" [Lowe, 2004] is performed in yet a different way compared to HOG and CCFMs, at least in the implementation of Vedaldi and Fulkerson [2008]. Compared to CCFMs, the bins on the boundary are let away. If disregarding explicit weighting by magnitudes or a spatial window, the CCFM follows the paradigm that each measurement should have equal weight in the histogram ("equal out" for observations), whereas the SIFT descriptor is designed such that all bins get the same number and weight of observations ("equal in" for bins); see Figure 4.5.

Thus, the SIFT descriptor can be computed as a CCFM in a similar way as the HOG descriptor (4.7)

$$\mathrm{CCFM}(n_1, n_2, n_3) = \sum_{(i,j)\in\mathcal{T}[\Omega]} g(i, j)|\nabla I(i, j)| \prod_{l=1}^{3} K_{\mathrm{B}}(x_l(i, j) - n_l + 1) , \qquad (4.8)$$

where $\mathcal{T}[\Omega]$ is the transformed image patch around the keypoint with orientation $\theta_0$, the numbers of bins $n_1, n_2 \in \{2, 3\}$, $n_3 \in \{1, \ldots, 8\}$, and $x_3(i, j) = \frac{4}{\pi}(\theta(i, j) - \theta_0)$.

Note that this formulation (as well as the CCFM-HOG (4.7)) can easily be extended to include color information. Color can be represented in various ways using regular channel representations of parametric color models such as RGB, HSV, or L*a*b*. Alternatively, learned, irregular representations such as color names as suggested by Van De Weijer et al. [2009] can be used.

The mathematical formulation is very similar in all cases, but in the subsequent example we follow the suggestion by Felsberg and Hedborg [2007b] to apply the HSV color space.

To form a CCFM with color information, the value (V) component is used to compute the gradient orientation and a potential weighting by the gradient magnitude. The hue (H) and saturation (S) components are used as two additional dimensions $x_4$ and $x_5$. Note that the hue $h \in [0; 2\pi)$ is periodic whereas saturation $s \in [0; 1]$ is not. Thus, for $N_4 = N_5 = 8$,

$$x_4(i, j) = \frac{4}{\pi} h \tag{4.9}$$
$$x_5(i, j) = 7s \tag{4.10}$$

and we apply (4.3) with $K_B$, $d = 3$, and $\xi_{l,n_l} = n_l - 1$. The CCFM versions of a color-SIFT and a color-HOG are obtained by computing the product over $l = 1, \ldots, 5$ in (4.8) and (4.7), respectively. For the SIFT-case, a comparison of the discriminative power of SIFT (applied to RGB separately) a color-based CCFMs has been performed by Felsberg and Hedborg [2007b].

The results of this comparison are illustrated in Figure 4.7. The task was to estimate the camera pose (position and orientation) $\mathbf{p} = [p_1\ p_2\ p_3\ r_1\ r_2\ r_3]^T$ from the feature vector $\mathbf{c}$ of the corresponding scene view. The task is addressed by a simple (supervised) machine learning approach, where a set of views and poses are given as training data. The validation is then done on a separate set of views and in two settings.

In the first, discrete setting (D), the output is the previously seen training sample that is closest, i.e., the pose of the nearest neighbor is reported. In the second, continuous setting (C), the output is an interpolated pose, generated from the training poses.

Following the concept of linkage matrices as suggested by Granlund [2000b], a linear mapping $\mathbf{M}$ from feature vectors to pose vectors is to be optimized, such that the pose estimate becomes $\hat{\mathbf{p}} = \mathbf{Mc}$. The training samples for $\mathbf{p}^{(m)}$ and $\mathbf{c}^{(m)}$ (column vectors) are arranged to form the matrices $\mathbf{P}$ and $\mathbf{C}$, respectively.

Obviously, $\mathbf{M}$ has significantly more degrees of freedom than the number of training samples, and thus we have to solve a constrained minimization problem. Usually, minimizing the number of non-zero entries in $\mathbf{M}$ could be achieved by minimizing the $L_1$-norm, but more efficient algorithms are available for the Frobenius norm:

$$\hat{\mathbf{M}} = \arg\min_{\mathbf{M} \in \mathcal{S}} \|\mathbf{M}\|_F^2 \ , \mathcal{S} = \left\{\mathbf{M} \in \mathbb{R}^{M \times N}; \mathbf{P} = \mathbf{MC}\right\} \ . \tag{4.11}$$

The explicit solution is obtained by the pseudo inverse $\mathbf{C}^\dagger$ of $\mathbf{C}$ [Farnebäck, 1999]

$$\hat{\mathbf{M}} = \mathbf{PC}^\dagger \ . \tag{4.12}$$

The interpolated pose (continuous mode C) for a feature vector $\mathbf{c}$ is obtained using the explicit solution

$$\hat{\mathbf{p}} = \hat{\mathbf{M}}\mathbf{c} = \mathbf{PC}^\dagger\mathbf{c} = \mathbf{P}\left(\mathbf{C}^\dagger\mathbf{c}\right) \ . \tag{4.13}$$

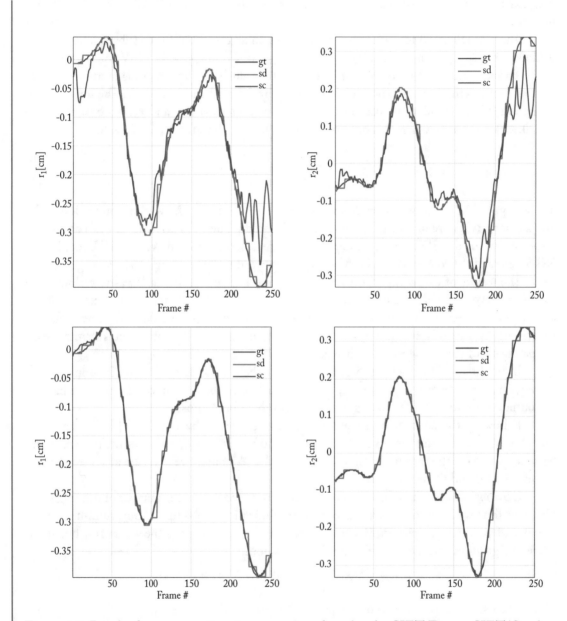

Figure 4.7: Results from pose estimation: gt—ground truth, sd—SIFT/D, sc—SIFT/C, cd—CCFM/D, and cc—CCFM/C. D and C refer to discrete and continuous, respectively. Figure based on Felsberg and Hedborg [2007b].

From the last equality we can see that the interpolation is a linear function of the training poses $\mathbf{p}^{(m)}$. The pose with the largest interprolation coefficient is considered to be the nearest neighbor in the training set. This pose (discrete mode D) for a feature vector $\mathbf{c}$ is obtained as

$$\hat{\mathbf{p}} = \mathbf{p}^{(\hat{m})} \;,\; \text{where} \quad \hat{m} = \arg\max_{m} \left( \mathbf{C}^{\dagger}\mathbf{c} \right)_{m} \;. \tag{4.14}$$

The interpolated solution in (4.13) can be considered as an attempt to map the index distribution over $m$, computed as $\mathbf{C}^{\dagger}\mathbf{c}$, to the pose space. The inverse interpretation would be that the pose estimate $\hat{\mathbf{p}}$ has a corresponding channel representation, which is estimated by the index distribution $\mathbf{C}^{\dagger}\mathbf{c}$. Thus, the interpolation in (4.13) can be considered as a channel *decoding*, which directly leads to the topic of the subsequent chapter.

## 4.4    THE SHOT DESCRIPTOR AS A CCFM

The so far discussed descriptor and feature map formulations have been addressing image features, i.e., 2D spatial domains. With the increasingly popular low-cost range sensors, interest in distinctive, yet geometrically invariant, descriptors for 3D features has grown. One of the most recent and discriminative descriptors is the *signature of histograms of orientations* (SHOT) descriptor by Salti et al. [2014].

According to its authors, the SHOT descriptor combines properties of a signature-based descriptor with those of a histogram-based descriptor, but the SHOT descriptor differs from other combined descriptors such as RoPS, proposed by Guo et al. [2013], because it is also suggested in a color-version. In that sense, it is similar to MeshHoG as proposed by Zaharescu et al. [2012], but with a more robust estimation of the reference frame as pointed out by Salti et al. [2014].

Relative to the reference frame, the SHOT-algorithm divides the 3D volume in $8 \times 2 \times 2 = 32$ cells, eight bins for azimuths, 2 for elevation, and 2 for the radius. Azimuth and elevation are periodic values, the radius is linear with bin centers at $R/4$ and $3R/4$ where $R$ is the maximum radius of the 3D volume. Thus, at the origin and at the maximum radius $R$, the radius weight is 0.5, similar to HOG, see (4.7).

The values that are encoded in the histogram part are the normal vectors representing the shape, and, in the color version, L*a*b* color-vectors. The shape-part of the histogram consists of the cosine of the angle between the reference normal and the normal in the point, calculated by the scalar product between the vectors, binned into 11 bins. The color-part of the histogram consists of $L_1$-distances between the reference L*a*b* vector and the L*a*b* vector in the point, binned into 31 bins.[2]

---

[2]The bin counts are inconsistent between the paper and the PCL implementation (http://docs.ros.org/hydro/api/pcl/html/shot_8hpp_source.html#l00836) of SHOT. The paper suggests 11 shape bins and 30 color bins and an inconsistent descriptor length of 1,280, whereas PCL suggests a descriptor length of 1,344, corresponding to 11 shape bins and 31 color bins.

The 3D cell array and the histogram part (shape or shape + color) form a 4D array, such that the processing described above corresponds to a quadrilinear interpolation. In other words, the SHOT descriptor is basically a 4D channel representation, or CCFM with $3 + 1$ dimensions.

Of the four dimensions, two are periodic dimensions (azimuth $x_1 = \omega$ and elevation $x_2 = \phi$) and two are linear dimensions (radius $x_3 = d$ and cosines of normals $x_4 = \theta$):

$$\mathrm{CCFM}(n_1, n_2, n_3, n_4) = \sum_{i:x_3(i)\leq R} \prod_{l=1}^{4} K_\mathrm{B}(x_l(i) - n_l + 1) \tag{4.15}$$

with indices $n_1 \in \{1, \ldots, 8\}, n_2, n_3 \in \{1, \ldots, 2\}, n_4 \in \{1, \ldots, 11\}$.

For color SHOT (CSHOT), the fourth dimension is concatenated using $x_4 = \|\Delta_{\mathrm{L^*a^*b^*}}\|_1$ for $n_4 \in \{12, \ldots, 42\}$; see Figure 4.8. The descriptor (4.15) is normalized such that $\|\mathrm{CCFM}(n_1, n_2, n_3, n_4)\|_2 = 1$. In CSHOT, the color part is normalized separately.

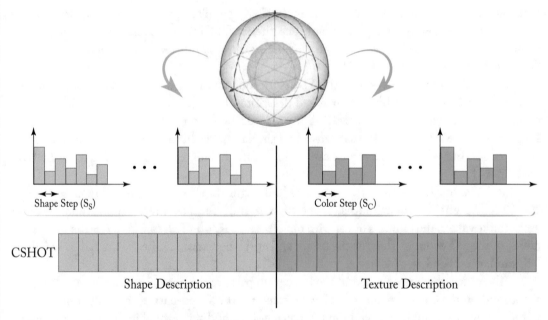

Figure 4.8: For each cell in the sphere (here only four azimuth cells), the shape and color descriptors are concatenated. Figure based on Salti et al. [2014].

The proper normalization of the descriptor is by no means obvious. Following the reasoning in Öfjäll and Felsberg [2017], the two different radial shells should have different weights, compensating for the change of volume. Otherwise a decoding of the descriptor, see Chapter 5, will lead to a result biased toward the outer radius. However, a decoding or visualization has not been the primary focus of the original SHOT descriptor paper by Salti et al. [2014] and no weighting has been suggested.

## SUMMARY

In this chapter we have discussed CCFMs and their relation to SIFT and HOG (2D) and SHOT (3D). It turns out that any of these three descriptors can be computed as CCFMs. In some cases, the CCFM needs to be computed in a reference frame (SIFT, SHOT), sometimes additional weighting is required (HOG, SIFT). Normalization is commonly applied. Many other descriptors that are based on signatures, histograms, or combinations of both can also be computed as CCFMs; for instance 2D SURF [Bay et al., 2008], 3D SURF [Knopp et al., 2010], MeshHoG [Zaharescu et al., 2012], and RoPS [Guo et al., 2013]. In the next chapter we will now focus on the technical details of channel decoding, reflecting on several decoding paradigms and also on the relations to visualization of other feature descriptors.

# CHAPTER 5

# CCFM Decoding and Visualization

The CCFMs as introduced in the previous chapter are not just a powerful feature representation generalizing other popular descriptors, but also allow for the extraction of robust estimates. For instance, the pose vector estimates described previously or the results from channel smoothing (see Figure 5.1) are obtained by the *decoding of CCFMs*, which is the central topic of this chapter.

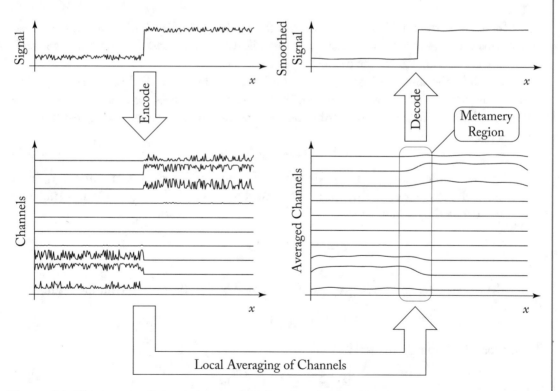

Figure 5.1: Illustration of channel smoothing: the noisy signal (left) is smoothed without blurring the edge (right). This is achieved by spatial averaging of the channels, leading to a metamery region. Illustration by Felsberg and Granlund [2003].

Decoding can be based on the maximum likelihood approach or the maximum entropy principle. For the descriptor identities formulated in the previous chapter, the decoding competes with the respective feature visualization approach.

## 5.1   CHANNEL DECODING

Various ways to decode channel representations for different kernels have been suggested in the past, e.g., by Forssén [2004] and Felsberg et al. [2006]. Obviously, the methodology for decoding depends on the chosen kernel. For rectangular kernels, i.e., ordinary histograms (3.3), no decoding with sub-bin accuracy can be achieved. Decoding becomes simply a nearest neighbor approach, where the bin center of the strongest bin is returned.

Histograms with rectangular kernels can be post-processed by smoothing the bins (as done by, e.g., Sevilla-Lara and Learned-Miller [2012]) or fitting a curve to several bins (as done for extracting the main orientation according to Lowe [2004]), but in all cases the output will be biased by the relative placement of the distribution mode and the bin centers [Felsberg et al., 2015].

In all cases, the actual goal is to estimate the mode of the distribution over the encoded entity. This estimate should be robust, with low bias (high accuracy) and low variance (high precision); see Section 2.1 for the definitions of these terms.

To model the three statistical properties of accuracy, precision, and robustness, consider a feature distribution $p_f$ and an outlier distribution $p_o$. Observations are then drawn from the convex combination of these two distributions, where the parameter $\lambda \in [0; 1)$ depends on the outlier rate:

$$x^{(m)} \sim (1 - \lambda)p_f + \lambda p_o \ . \tag{5.1}$$

Assume further that $p_f$ has a maximum $x_0$. The goal of decoding is to estimate $x_0$ from $\mathbf{c}$, the channel encoding of the samples $x^{(m)}$ according to ((3.3)/(3.9)/(3.10)). The encoding operator is denoted by $\mathcal{C}$ in what follows, i.e.:

$$\mathbf{c} = M^{-1} \sum_m \mathcal{C}\left(x^{(m)}\right) \ . \tag{5.2}$$

The corresponding decoding operator is denoted by $\mathcal{C}^\dagger$. Thus, we obtain the estimate of the maximum $x_0$ as

$$\hat{x}_0 = \mathcal{C}^\dagger(\mathbf{c}) \ . \tag{5.3}$$

The estimate is absolutely robust if

$$\mathrm{E}[\hat{x}_0]_{p_f} = \mathrm{E}[\hat{x}_0]_{(1-\lambda)p_f + \lambda p_o} \ , \tag{5.4}$$

the estimated mode is independent of the outlier rate and the outlier distribution. In practice, this can only be achieved if the outlier rate is limited and if the distribution does not have strong maxima itself, i.e., if the outlier distribution is close to uniform.

What exactly is meant by *limited outlier rate* and *close to uniform* depends on the application; outlier rate and outlier distribution are empirical entities and given those entities, (5.4) must hold to make the estimate robust.

The accuracy is defined in terms of the bias of the estimate. Given the previously introduced notation, the bias is given as

$$\text{BIAS}[\hat{x}_0] = \text{E}[\hat{x}_0] - x_0 \ . \tag{5.5}$$

Note that a necessary (but not sufficient) requirement for an unbiased estimate from a CCFM is that the bias of the kernel density estimate in (3.15) is zero

$$\arg\max_x \int_{-\infty}^{\infty} p(x')K(x' - x)\, dx' = x_0 \ . \tag{5.6}$$

If the kernel is symmetric, as assumed throughout this text, this implies that the density $p$ must be symmetric in the support of $K(x - x_0)$. Therefore, smaller kernels are more likely to lead to unbiased estimates also for the channel decoding. The bias introduced by lack of symmetry in the density is by far smaller than the bias introduced by unsuitable kernels or decoding schemes. Thus, we assume local symmetry of the density in the subsequent considerations.

For histograms with rectangular bins (3.3) and under this symmetry assumption, the bias is the negative difference to the integer value of the maximum, $[x_0]$:

$$\text{BIAS}[\hat{x}_0] = [x_0] - x_0 \ . \tag{5.7}$$

If the maximum $x_0$ is drawn from a uniform distribution, the expectation of the bias modulus is $1/4$.

For linear kernels (3.9) one would expect a reduced bias compared to rectangular kernels due to the higher order of the kernel. However, combinations of linear B-splines nearly always attend their extrema on the nodes, i.e., $[x_0]$. The only exception to this is if two neighbored coefficients are exactly equal, such that the B-spline becomes horizontal. Except for this singular event, the bias for linear B-spline estimates is the same as for the rectangular bins.

For the $\cos^2$-kernel, two different paradigms have been developed, one based on maximization of entropy [Jonsson and Felsberg, 2005] and one based on frame theory [Forssén, 2004]. Both have zero bias but differ in precision. Frame theory allows for the movement of energy, thus squared errors, between domains. Thus, the frame theory approach leads to minimal variance, i.e., highest precision. Entropy, on the other hand, is an information-theoretic measure. Maximum entropy decoding thus leads to the solution with the least coded information (fewest local maxima) even if at the cost of reduced precision.

To illustrate the use of channel decoding, we consider the method to speed-up bilateral filtering of images by means of channel smoothing [Felsberg et al., 2006], [Paris and Durand, 2006], and [Kass and Solomon, 2010]. Bilateral filtering allows for the denoising of a signal or an image without blurring edges because the different intensity/color levels on the two sides of the edge are represented in different parts of the model. Thus, the two levels are not confused and close to the edge a metamery region is formed. The finally decoded value is picked based on the majority of observations in the spatial neighborhood; see Figure 5.1.

The robustness of channel smoothing is not restricted to intensity/color, but can be used on any type of feature map, e.g., local orientation [Felsberg et al., 2006]. Furthermore, the statistics of the observed feature distribution can be used to further control the smoothing process: the noise level can be used to derive a Wiener filter, i.e., control the width of the filter [Felsberg, 2005], and the local orientation can be used to steer oriented filters—acting on the orientation field [Felsberg and Granlund, 2004] or across modalities on the intensity [Felsberg and Granlund, 2003].

## 5.2   DECODING BASED ON FRAME THEORY

The approach based on frame theory has been considered for varying degrees of overlap and for two different confidence measures. In this text, we limit ourselves to the minimum overlap case (three according to Felsberg et al. [2015]) and describe the proposed maximum likelihood decoding, which combines the confidence measures suggested by Forssén [2004].

The first step in decoding a channel vector $\mathbf{c}$ is to select an index $n$, which will be the center of the decoding window (of width three)

$$\mathbf{c} = [\dots, c_{n-2}, \underbrace{c_{n-1}, c_n, c_{n+1}}_{\text{decoding window}}, c_{n+2}, \dots]^{\mathrm{T}} \; . \tag{5.8}$$

How to select this index will be explained below.

By rotating the three-vector in the decoding window $\mathbf{c}_n = [c_{n-1}, c_n, c_{n+1}]^{\mathrm{T}}$, we obtain the $\mathbf{p}_n$ vector, which is parametrized in $(r_n, s_n, \alpha_n)$

$$\begin{bmatrix} r_n \cos(\alpha_n) \\ r_n \sin(\alpha_n) \\ s_n \end{bmatrix} =: \mathbf{p}_n = \frac{1}{\sqrt{3}} \begin{bmatrix} \sqrt{2} & \sqrt{2}\cos(2\pi/3) & \sqrt{2}\cos(4\pi/3) \\ 0 & \sqrt{2}\sin(2\pi/3) & \sqrt{2}\sin(4\pi/3) \\ 1 & 1 & 1 \end{bmatrix} \mathbf{c}_n \; . \tag{5.9}$$

These parameters establish the triple of evidence $s_n$, coherence $r_n/s_n$, and value $\alpha_n$ [Felsberg et al., 2015]; see Figure 5.2.

Usually, $\alpha_n \in [\pi/3; \pi]$ but if $\alpha_n$ is outside that range, $r_n$ needs to be modified using

$$r_n \leftarrow r_n \cos(|\alpha_n - 2\pi/3| - \pi/3) \; . \tag{5.10}$$

We then select the decoding window according to

$$\hat{n} = \arg\max_n r_n + \sqrt{2}s_n \; . \tag{5.11}$$

The corresponding decoded value

$$\hat{x} = \max\left(\min\left(\frac{3}{2\pi}(\alpha_{\hat{n}} - 2\pi/3), \frac{1}{2}\right), -\frac{1}{2}\right) + \hat{n} \tag{5.12}$$

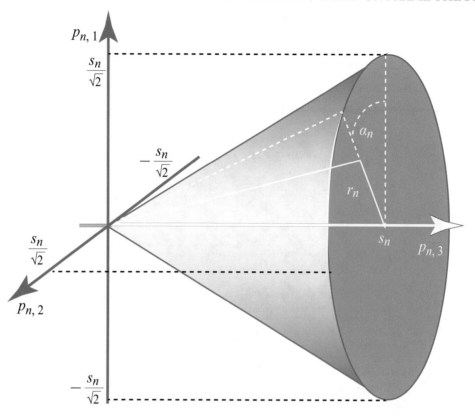

Figure 5.2: The 3D cone formed by evidence $s_n$, coherence $r_n/s_n$, and value $\alpha_n$. Based on Felsberg et al. [2015].

is the maximum likelihood estimate (MLE) given $\mathbf{c}$ and assuming independent noise, as it has been shown by Felsberg et al. [2015]:

$$\hat{x} = \arg \max_x p(x|\mathbf{c}) = \arg \min_x \left\| [K(x - \xi_1), \dots, K(x - \xi_N)]^{\mathrm{T}} - \mathbf{c} \right\|_2^2 . \tag{5.13}$$

This result is verified by a Monte Carlo simulation in Figure 5.3.

The observation that (5.12) is the maximum likelihood estimator is quite remarkable. It means that a nonlinear optimization problem is solved without numerical calculation of gradients.

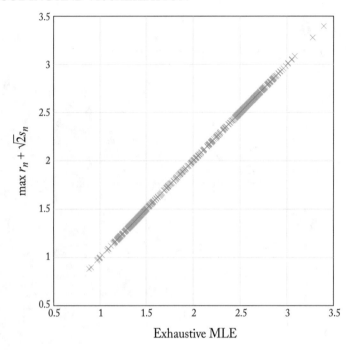

Figure 5.3: Comparison between exhaustive search of the MLE and the MLE according to (5.13). 1,000 random measurements have been generated with random weights and encoded with 7 channels. Figure based on Felsberg et al. [2015]

Another interesting observations done by Öfjäll and Felsberg [2014b] is that the (squared) coherence of a channel vector can be computed by a ratio of bilinear forms:

$$\text{coh}^2(\mathbf{c}_n) = \frac{r_n^2}{s_n^2} = \frac{1}{\mathbf{1}^{\text{T}} \mathbf{c}_n \mathbf{c}_n^{\text{T}} \mathbf{1}} \mathbf{c}_n^{\text{T}} \begin{bmatrix} 4 & -2 & -2 \\ -2 & 4 & -2 \\ -2 & -2 & 4 \end{bmatrix} \mathbf{c}_n \ . \tag{5.14}$$

Despite all its useful properties, the MLE assumes solely one value to be shaping the distribution. Hence, in metamery regions, the alternative interpretations will confuse the MLE and multi-modal estimation is impossible. This is different for the maximum entropy decoding.

## 5.3   MAXIMUM ENTROPY DECODING

In contrast to the decoding as suggested above, just obtaining the mode of the distribution, maximum entropy decoding according to Jonsson and Felsberg [2005] attempts to extract the whole distribution. The idea is to find the simplest, i.e., the least informative, distribution that fits the channel coefficients. The simplest distribution maximizes the differential entropy

$$H(p) = -\int_{-\infty}^{\infty} p(x) \log p(x) \, dx \ . \tag{5.15}$$

Fitting the channel coefficients is guaranteed by the constraints

$$\int_{-\infty}^{\infty} p(x) K(x - \xi_n) \, dx \ = \ c_n, \qquad 1 \leq n \leq N \tag{5.16}$$

$$\int_{-\infty}^{\infty} p(x) \, dx \ = \ 1 \ . \tag{5.17}$$

Using a variational approach with Lagrange multipliers $\lambda_n$, $0 \leq n \leq N$, we obtain

$$p(x) = \exp \lambda_0 \exp \left( \sum_{n=1}^{N} \lambda_n K(x - \xi_n) \right) \ . \tag{5.18}$$

To the best of our knowledge, the explicit solution of $\lambda_n$ cannot be calculated and Jonsson and Felsberg [2005] have suggested to apply a Newton method using numerical evaluations of the integrals on a very fine grid. Obviously, this comes with an enormous efficiency penalty and is thus only interesting for single simulations.

In order to improve efficiency, Öfjäll and Felsberg [2017] suggest approximating the differential entropy as used in previous work by Jonsson and Felsberg [2005] using the linear Taylor expansion of the logarithm in (5.15)

$$H_2(p) = \int_{-\infty}^{\infty} \frac{3}{2} p(x)(1 - p(x)) \, dx \ . \tag{5.19}$$

This objective is maximized under the same constraints (5.16) and (5.17). Using a variational approach with Lagrange multipliers $\lambda_n$, $0 \leq n \leq N$, we obtain:

$$p(x) = \frac{\lambda_0}{3} + \frac{1}{2} + \frac{1}{3} \sum_{n=1}^{N} \lambda_n K(x - \xi_n). \tag{5.20}$$

Note the finite support of $K$ and the infinite integration in (5.17) imply $\lambda_0 = -\frac{3}{2}$. Thus, the first two terms in (5.20) cancel out and we will skip $\lambda_0$ in what follows.

In contrast to previous work by Jonsson and Felsberg [2005], (5.20) can be directly inserted into (5.16), resulting in:

$$
\begin{aligned}
c_n &= \int_{-\infty}^{\infty} \left( \frac{1}{3} \sum_{n'=1}^{N} \lambda_{n'} K(x - \xi_{n'}) \right) K(x - \xi_n)\, dx, \qquad 1 \le n \le N \\
&= \frac{1}{3} \sum_{n'=1}^{N} \lambda_{n'} \int_{-\infty}^{\infty} K(x - \xi_{n'}) K(x - \xi_n)\, dx, \qquad 1 \le n \le N \\
&= \frac{1}{3} \sum_{n'=1}^{N} \lambda_{n'} \begin{cases} \frac{1}{2} & n = n' \\ \frac{1}{6} + \frac{\sqrt{3}}{8\pi} & n = n' \pm 1, \\ \frac{1}{12} - \frac{\sqrt{3}}{8\pi} & n = n' \pm 2 \end{cases} \qquad 1 \le n \le N \\
&= \frac{1}{3} \left( \left( \frac{1}{12} - \frac{\sqrt{3}}{8\pi} \right) (\lambda_{n+2} + \lambda_{n-2}) + \right. \\
&\qquad \left. + \left( \frac{1}{6} + \frac{\sqrt{3}}{8\pi} \right) (\lambda_{n+1} + \lambda_{n-1}) + \frac{\lambda_n}{2} \right), \qquad 1 \le n \le N,
\end{aligned}
$$

where $\lambda_n = 0$ if $n < 1$ or $n > N$.

Note that $\mathbf{c}$ is obtained from $\boldsymbol{\lambda} = [\lambda_1, \ldots, \lambda_N]^{\mathrm{T}}$ by a discrete linear filter such that the sums of components behave as

$$
\sum_{n=1}^{N} c_n = \frac{1}{3} \sum_{n=1}^{N} \lambda_n . \tag{5.21}
$$

Thus, a normalized $\mathbf{c}$ implies that the sum of Lagrange multipliers $\boldsymbol{\lambda}$ is 3, an easy to verify constraint. To obtain $\boldsymbol{\lambda}$, solve the linear system

$$
\mathbf{A}\boldsymbol{\lambda} = \mathbf{c}, \tag{5.22}
$$

where

$$
\mathbf{A} = \frac{1}{3} \begin{bmatrix}
\frac{1}{2} & \frac{1}{6} + \frac{\sqrt{3}}{8\pi} & \frac{1}{12} - \frac{\sqrt{3}}{8\pi} & 0 & \cdots & & & 0 \\
\frac{1}{6} + \frac{\sqrt{3}}{8\pi} & \ddots & \ddots & \ddots & \ddots & & & \vdots \\
\frac{1}{12} - \frac{\sqrt{3}}{8\pi} & \ddots & \ddots & \ddots & \ddots & & & 0 \\
0 & \ddots & \ddots & \ddots & \ddots & & \frac{1}{12} - \frac{\sqrt{3}}{8\pi} & \\
\vdots & \ddots & \ddots & \ddots & \ddots & & \frac{1}{6} + \frac{\sqrt{3}}{8\pi} & \\
0 & \cdots & 0 & \frac{1}{12} - \frac{\sqrt{3}}{8\pi} & \frac{1}{6} + \frac{\sqrt{3}}{8\pi} & \frac{1}{2}
\end{bmatrix} . \tag{5.23}
$$

Once the coefficients $\lambda_n$ are determined from (5.22), we can exploit (5.20) to compute necessary conditions for local maxima $x_0$ by requiring a vanishing first derivative and a negative second derivative, i.e.,

$$p'(x_0) = \frac{1}{3}\sum_{n=1}^{N}\lambda_n K'(x_0 - \xi_n) = 0 \tag{5.24}$$

$$p''(x_0) = \frac{1}{3}\sum_{n=1}^{N}\lambda_n K''(x_0 - \xi_n) < 0 \ . \tag{5.25}$$

From (3.8) we determine

$$K'(x) = \begin{cases} -\frac{4\pi}{9}\sin(2\pi x/3) & |x| \le 3/2 \\ 0 & \text{otherwise} \end{cases} \tag{5.26}$$

$$K''(x) = \begin{cases} -\frac{8\pi^2}{27}\cos(2\pi x/3) & |x| \le 3/2 \\ 0 & \text{otherwise} \end{cases} . \tag{5.27}$$

Instead of inverting the matrix (5.23), we derive a recursive filter that traverses the channel vector **c** forth and back, similar to the decoding method for B-spline kernels as suggested by Felsberg et al. [2006]. We start looking at the $z$-transform of the filter realized by (5.23) (defining $a = \frac{1}{3} - \frac{\sqrt{3}}{2\pi}$)

$$H(z) = \frac{az^{-2} + (1-a)z^{-1} + 2 + (1-a)z + az^2}{12} \tag{5.28}$$

and thus we obtain

$$\begin{aligned} H^{-1} &= \frac{12z^{-2}}{a + (1-a)z^{-1} + 2z^{-2} + (1-a)z^{-3} + az^{-4}} \\ &= \frac{12}{a}\frac{1}{z^{-2} - z_1 z^{-1} + 1}\frac{z^{-2}}{z^{-2} - z_2 z^{-1} + 1}, \end{aligned} \tag{5.29}$$

where

$$z_{1/2} = \frac{1}{2} - \frac{1}{2a} \pm \frac{\sqrt{a^{-2} - 10a^{-1} + 9}}{2} \ . \tag{5.30}$$

Hence, we get the following recursions:

$$c_n^+ = c_n + z_1 c_{n-1}^+ - c_{n-2}^+ \qquad (n = 3, \dots, N) \tag{5.31}$$

$$c_n^- = c_n^+ + z_2 c_{n+1}^- - c_{n+2}^- \qquad (n = N-2, \dots, 1) \tag{5.32}$$

$$\lambda_n = \frac{12}{a}c_n^- \qquad (n = 1, \dots, N) \ . \tag{5.33}$$

It has been assumed that $c_n = 0$ for $n < 1$ or $n > N$. Therefore, the initial conditions of the filters are[1]

$$
\begin{aligned}
c_1^+ &= c_1 & (5.34)\\
c_2^+ &= c_2 + z_1 c_1 & (5.35)\\
c_N^- &= c_N^+ & (5.36)\\
c_{N-1}^- &= c_{N-1}^+ + z_2 c_N^+. & (5.37)
\end{aligned}
$$

In contrast to (5.18), which is non-negative by design, negative $\lambda_n$ might lead to (5.20) violating the non-negativity property of density functions and a separate consideration of this property is required, as pointed out by Öfjäll and Felsberg [2017].

The maximum entropy decoding appears quite complex, but it is computationally efficient and returns an estimate of the complete distribution in terms of coefficients $\lambda$. In contrast, typical de-featuring methods for visualizing other descriptors such as HOG and SIFT return only single values per pixel and are rather ad-hoc, as described in the subsequent section.

## 5.4   RELATION TO OTHER DE-FEATURING METHODS

The problem of de-featuring, i.e., decoding feature descriptors, has been addressed frequently in recent work. Besides the previously considered features, i.e., for SIFT [Weinzaepfel et al., 2011] and HOG [Vondrick et al., 2013], also deep features [Mahendran and Vedaldi, 2015, Zeiler and Fergus, 2014] as well as quantized descriptors, such as LBP [d'Angelo et al., 2012] and BOV [Kato and Harada, 2014] have been addressed.

In this section, we will focus on SIFT and HOG because we have derived their corresponding formulations with CCFMs in Chapter 4. The main difference between the two de-featuring methods by Weinzaepfel et al. [2011] and Vondrick et al. [2013] is that HOG features are computed densely over an image region, whereas SIFT features are located at detected keypoints and at the respective scale.

Thus, the de-featuring of HOG (*HOGgles*) is a process on a regular grid and we start by explaining the underlying idea. In a first step, sets of images are extracted from a large database, where the elements of each set are associated with the same descriptor, but are pairwise diverse. In terms of invariance properties, the elements in each set are invariant under the HOG descriptor.

Algorithmically, over-complete bases (frames) are use for representing the images from the dataset and the respective descriptors as linear combinations. The key of the approach is that the coefficients of the two linear combinations are shared and link the descriptors to the respective images; see Figure 5.4.

The diversity of images leads to a Tikhonov regularization of the linear coefficients. The coefficients are further required to be sparse by exploiting an $L_1$-penalty. Thus, the HOGgles

---

[1]Note that the boundary conditions (5.36–5.37) are nontrivial: due to the instability of the filters, numerical results might differ. However, we know from our assumptions that all $\lambda_n = 0$ for $n < 1$ or $n > N$ and thus $c_n = 0$ for $n > N$.

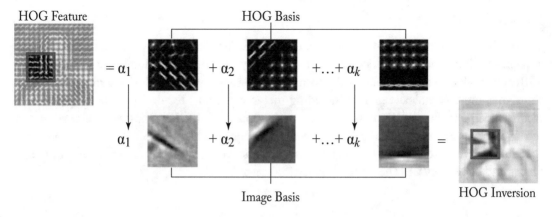

Figure 5.4: The approach is based on two frames (bases), one for the descriptor and one for the image. The coefficients are shared and form the reconstructed image. Figure based on Vondrick et al. [2013].

approach shares similarities with CCFM reconstruction based on frame theory (see Section 5.2), orientation scores (see Section 3.3), and with sparse coding [Olshausen and Field, 1997].

The main difference to CCFM reconstruction is that the latter aims at reconstructing the complete orientation map, not the underlying image. The main difference to orientation scores is that the latter form a wavelet basis (tight frame). The main difference to sparse coding are the coefficients that are shared over two dictionaries (frames).

In contrast to de-featuring of HOG, the visualization of SIFT [Weinzaepfel et al., 2011] is based on image patch prototypes that are stitched together and interpolated. The focus of the method is on the stitching and interpolation, which are both topics beyond the scope of this text.

The patch prototypes are simply stored together with the respective feature vectors for a large dataset of images. For visualizing a local descriptor, the most similar descriptor prototype is identified and the associated image patch prototype is used for visualization.

Thus, the SIFT-based reconstruction is based on memorizing local patches and combining them in the image domain. This is quite different from CCFM reconstruction and HOGgles, mainly due to the irregular placement of the local feature descriptors. However, the algorithm requires the comparison between descriptors, and Weinzaepfel et al. [2011] propose to use the $L_2$-distance.

In the subsequent chapter we discuss the comparison of descriptors by means of probabilistic approaches and argue why the $L_2$-distance is less suitable than the $L_1$-distance and divergence-based distances.

## SUMMARY

In this chapter we have discussed the decoding of CCFMs based on two different approaches: a maximum likelihood estimation using frame theory and a maximum entropy reconstruction of the entire distribution. Whereas the former is real-time capable and works robustly in most situations, more complex scenarios including metamery might require the more sophisticated reconstruction of the distribution. The reconstruction from CCFMs has also been related to reconstructions from HOG and SIFT. In the subsequent chapter we will now focus on the probabilistic interpretation of channel representations, covering technical details of proper distances and dependency in the multi-dimensional case.

CHAPTER 6

# Probabilistic Interpretation of Channel Representations

The channel representation was originally introduced as a deterministic information representation concept, based on methods from signal processing and motivated by observation from biology (Granlund [2000*b*], Section 2.5). Due to its relation to histograms and kernel density estimators, connections to probabilistic interpretations have been identified in later years by Felsberg et al. [2006] and Duits, Felsberg, Granlund and ter Haar Romeny [2007].

In particular, the distribution of coefficient values can be considered in context of multinomial distributions and their divergences, also leading to a connection with categorical distributions and thus symbolic (discrete) spaces. Finally, concepts like stochastic independence and Copulas are considered.

## 6.1    ON THE DISTRIBUTION OF CHANNEL VALUES

Starting from the observation of channel representations being soft histograms, see Section 2.4, we build the subsequent consideration on the statistics of histograms, i.e., channel representations with rectangular kernels (3.2). Each of the bins corresponds to counting the appearance of an event, namely the value falling inside of a certain interval.

If we now assume that the event for each bin has a certain probability $P_n \geq 0$ such that $\sum_{n=1}^{N} P_n = 1$ and that the events of choosing bins are independent, we obtain a multinomial distribution with parameters $M$ (the number of trials) and $\mathbf{P} = (P_1, \ldots, P_N)$; see Evans et al. [2000].

From the literature we know that the expectation of histogram bin/channel coefficient $c_n$ is given as

$$\mathrm{E}[c_n] = M P_n \tag{6.1}$$

and (co-)variances of bins/channels are

$$\mathrm{var}[c_n] = M P_n (1 - P_n) \qquad \mathrm{cov}[c_n, c_{n'}] = -M P_n P_{n'} \ . \tag{6.2}$$

Thus, for large numbers of trials, the normalized channel coefficients $c_n / M$ can be used as approximate estimates of the probabilities. The variance is minimal for extreme cases (very small or very large coefficients) and covariances are always negative, meaning that if a trials falls into one bin, the expectation for the other bins is reduced.

Interestingly, there is geometric interpretation of multinomial distributions in terms of (generalized) barycentric coordinates, i.e., multi-dimensional equilateral pyramids; see Figure 6.1. The cases of small variance are those close to the corners of the pyramid, closely related to the case of distinct intrinsic dimensionality in Felsberg et al. [2009]. The pyramidal structure stems from the fact that $\mathbf{P}$ is an element of the probability simplex $\mathcal{S}_N$.

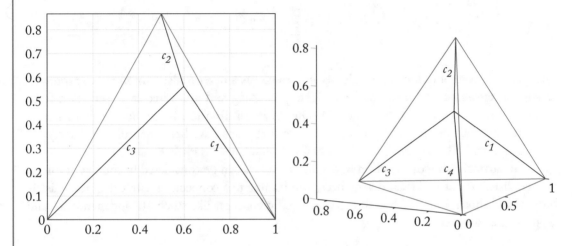

Figure 6.1: Illustration of multidimensional simplexes in 2D and 3D. The 1D simplex is just the interval [0; 1] on the real line. The 2D simplex is what is commonly called barycentric coordinates, a triangle parametrized by three values $(c_1, c_2, c_3)$ with unit sum. In 3D, we obtain a tetrahedron, parametrized with four values $(c_1, \ldots, c_4)$. Higher-dimensional cases can be illustrated only as animations, e.g., 4D simplex http://liu.diva-portal.org/smash/get/div a2:916645/MOVIE02.mp4.

The likelihood to observe the channel vector $\mathbf{c}$ is given by drawing

$$M = \sum_{n=1}^{N} c_n \qquad (6.3)$$

samples and distribute them in the $N$ bins, see Evans et al. [2000],

$$p(\mathbf{c}|\mathbf{P}, M) = \frac{M!}{\prod_{n=1}^{N} c_n!} \prod_{n=1}^{N} P_n^{c_n} = \frac{\Gamma(M+1)}{\prod_{n=1}^{N} \Gamma(c_n+1)} \prod_{n=1}^{N} P_n^{c_n} , \qquad (6.4)$$

where the Gamma function

$$\Gamma(s) = \int_0^{\infty} t^{s-1} \exp(-t) \, dt \qquad s \in \mathbb{R}^+ \qquad (6.5)$$

is the continuous generalization of the factorial function $(s-1)!$ for $s \in \mathbb{N}$.

Obviously, we are interested in the posterior rather than the likelihood and therefore we also have to consider the prior of the multinomial distribution. The conjugate prior of the multinomial distribution is the Dirichlet distribution

$$p(\mathbf{P}) = \text{Dir}(\mathbf{P}|\boldsymbol{\alpha}) = \frac{\Gamma(\sum_{n=1}^{N} \alpha_n)}{\prod_{n=1}^{N} \Gamma(\alpha_n)} \prod_{n=1}^{N} P_n^{\alpha_n-1} \quad, \tag{6.6}$$

where the concentration parameters $\boldsymbol{\alpha} = (\alpha_1, \ldots, \alpha_N)$ are positive reals and small values prefer sparse distributions [Hutter, 2013]. Since we do not have a reason to assume different initial concentrations for different bins, we consider the symmetric Dirichlet distribution as prior, i.e., $\alpha_1 = \ldots = \alpha_N = \alpha$,

$$\text{Dir}(\mathbf{P}|\alpha) = \frac{\Gamma(\alpha N)}{\Gamma(\alpha)^N} \prod_{n=1}^{N} P_n^{\alpha-1} \quad. \tag{6.7}$$

Thus, the posterior distribution $p(\mathbf{P}|\mathbf{c})$ is proportional to

$$p(\mathbf{c}|\mathbf{P})\text{Dir}(\mathbf{P}|\alpha) = \frac{\Gamma(M+1)}{\prod_{n=1}^{N} \Gamma(c_n+1)} \prod_{n=1}^{N} P_n^{c_n} \frac{\Gamma(\alpha N)}{\Gamma(\alpha)^N} \prod_{n=1}^{N} P_n^{\alpha-1} \tag{6.8}$$

$$= \frac{\Gamma(M+1)}{\prod_{n=1}^{N} \Gamma(c_n+1)} \frac{\Gamma(\sum_{n=1}^{N} \alpha)}{\prod_{n=1}^{N} \Gamma(\alpha)} \prod_{n=1}^{N} P_n^{c_n+\alpha-1} \tag{6.9}$$

$$\propto \frac{\Gamma(\sum_{n=1}^{N} c_n+\alpha)}{\prod_{n=1}^{N} \Gamma(c_n+\alpha)} \prod_{n=1}^{N} P_n^{c_n+\alpha-1} \tag{6.10}$$

$$= \text{Dir}(\mathbf{P}|\mathbf{c}+\alpha) \quad, \tag{6.11}$$

and the posterior distribution is a Dirichlet distribution with concentration parameter vector $\mathbf{c} + \alpha$. The posterior distribution is useful as it allows to compute divergences between histograms in statistically correct sense, from a Bayesian point of view; see Section 6.3.

From the posterior distribution we can compute the posterior predictive $p(\mathbf{c}'|\mathbf{c})$ by integrating the product of likelihood and posterior distribution over the probability simplex $\mathcal{S}_N$, resulting in a predicted histogram; see Section 6.2.

Finally, by integrating the posterior distribution over the probability simplex $\mathcal{S}_N$, we obtain the marginal distribution of the data, relevant for determining the correct Copula (in a Bayesian sense); see Section 6.4.

So far, we have only been considering histograms, i.e., rectangular kernel functions. Following the arguments of Scott [1992], the same statistical properties are obtained for linear interpolation between histogram bins. In the most general case, however, and in particular for the most useful kernels such as $\cos^2$, the correlation between neighbored bins violates the assumption about independent events for the respective bins.

A second problem are outliers that are located outside the channel representation: two channel representations might have the same coefficient vectors, but are generated from different numbers of samples. These additional samples must influence the posterior distribution.

The first problem requires a de-correlation of the coefficient vector, which is basically the problem solved in Section 5.3. The calculation of the coefficient vector in (5.22) consist mainly of solving the linear system with the channel correlation matrix as a system matrix. Consequently, the obtained coefficient vector $\lambda$ is a good approximation of independent events in the sense of a histogram. Thus, we replace $\mathbf{c}$ with $\lambda$ in (6.11).

Regarding the outliers, we simply add one further dimension corresponding to the range that is not covered by the channel representation. The de-correlation cannot be solved easily in this case, but we can assume that this additional dimension is independent of the other coefficients in the representation and therefore add the dimension directly to the de-correlated vector in terms of $\lambda_0$. The corresponding concentration parameter $\alpha_0$ is not necessarily identical to the other $\lambda$. For notational simplicity, we however stick to the direct formulation in terms of channel coefficient $c_n, n = 1, \ldots, N$ for the subsequent sections.

## 6.2  COMPARING CHANNEL REPRESENTATIONS

In many applications, the estimated distribution of measurements is only an intermediate step in some processing chain. In parameter regression problems, the subsequent step is to extract the modes of one distribution (see Chapter 5). In matching problems, two or more distributions need to be compared to produce matching scores.

The latter is, for instance, used in tracking as suggested by Felsberg [2013], where an appearance model is built over time, consisting of a channel coded feature map (see Chapter 4) that represents the empirical distribution of gray values over the tracking window. If a new frame is processed, candidate windows in the vicinity of the predicted position are to be compared to the existing model. The candidate window with the best score is chosen as the new object location; see Figure 6.2.

In the predecessor to the work of Felsberg [2013], Sevilla-Lara and Learned-Miller [2012] suggest using the $L_1$-distance to compare (smoothed) histograms, which is also applied for the channel-based tracker.

Obviously, it makes much more sense to use the $L_1$-distance between two channel vectors $\mathbf{c}$ and $\mathbf{c}'$

$$d_1(\mathbf{c}, \mathbf{c}') = \sum_{n=1}^{N} |c_n - c_n'| \tag{6.12}$$

or their Hellinger distance ($|\mathbf{c}|$ denotes the $L_1$-norm of $\mathbf{c}$)

$$H_{1/2}(\mathbf{c}, \mathbf{c}') = \frac{1}{2} \sum_{n=1}^{N} (\sqrt{c_n} - \sqrt{c_n'})^2 = \frac{|\mathbf{c}| + |\mathbf{c}'|}{2} - \sum_{n=1}^{N} \sqrt{c_n c_n'} \tag{6.13}$$

Figure 6.2: Applying channel representations for tracking as proposed by Felsberg [2013]. Left panel: current frame with tracked bounding box. Right panel, top: contents of the bounding box. Right panel, bottom: current model decoded (note the coarser representation in the occluded part).

instead of their $L_2$-distance, because channel coefficients are non-negative. The Hellinger distance has been introduced to channel representations through the use of the Bhattacharyya coefficient by Jonsson [2008], similar to the square-root transform on Fisher vectors [Sánchez et al., 2013].

The generalization of the Hellinger distance leads to comparisons my means of divergences; see Section 6.3. Before moving on to divergences where we consider the model coefficients and the new coefficients as representations of two distributions, we first consider the new coefficients in terms of a further likelihood term.

Similar to (6.11), we obtain a new Dirichlet distribution, which is then integrated out to obtain the posterior predictive (here computed for the uniform prior $\alpha = 1$)

$$p(\mathbf{c}'|\mathbf{c}) = \int p(\mathbf{c}'|\mathbf{P})\mathrm{Dir}(\mathbf{P}|\mathbf{c}+1)\,d\mathbf{P} \tag{6.14}$$

$$= \frac{\Gamma(|\mathbf{c}'|+1)\Gamma(|\mathbf{c}|+N)}{\prod_{n=1}^{N}\Gamma(c_n'+1)\Gamma(c_n+1)}\int \prod_{n=1}^{N} P_n^{(c_n+c_n'+1)-1}\,d\mathbf{P} \tag{6.15}$$

$$= \frac{\Gamma(|\mathbf{c}'|+1)\Gamma(|\mathbf{c}|+N)}{\Gamma(|\mathbf{c}|+|\mathbf{c}'|+N)}\prod_{n=1}^{N}\frac{\Gamma(c_n+c_n'+1)}{\Gamma(c_n'+1)\Gamma(c_n+1)} \tag{6.16}$$

$$= \frac{\Gamma(|\mathbf{c}'|+1)}{\Gamma(|\mathbf{c}'|+N)}\frac{B(\mathbf{c}+\mathbf{c}'+1)}{B(\mathbf{c}'+1)B(\mathbf{c}+1)}\ , \tag{6.17}$$

where $B()$ denotes the $N$-dimensional Beta function

$$B(\mathbf{c}) = \frac{\prod_{n=1}^{N}\Gamma(c_n)}{\Gamma(|\mathbf{c}|)}\ . \tag{6.18}$$

$B()$ is obtained by recursively applying the definition of the ordinary Beta function (see Evans et al. [2000]) that exist in many scientific computing programming libraries.

The first factor in (6.17) just depends on the number of bins and the number of draws, i.e., it is independent of the distribution and can be precomputed. The second factor is preferably computed in the logarithmic domain to avoid numerical problems.

Since the probability (6.17) is non-negative and bounded between 0 and 1, the negative logarithm results in a suitable distance measure

$$d_p(\mathbf{c}',\mathbf{c}) = -\log p(\mathbf{c}'|\mathbf{c}) \tag{6.19}$$

$$= \mathrm{gammaln}(|\mathbf{c}'|+N) - \mathrm{gammaln}(|\mathbf{c}'|+1) +$$
$$+ \mathrm{betaln}(\mathbf{c}'+1) + \mathrm{betaln}(\mathbf{c}+1) - \mathrm{betaln}(\mathbf{c}+\mathbf{c}'+1), \tag{6.20}$$

where gammaln() is the log-Gamma function and betaln() is the log-Beta function. Both exist in many scientific computing programming libraries.

In practice, the observed data often contains outliers and if we assume the coefficient vector $\mathbf{c}$ represents a convex combination of the true distribution and a uniform distribution, with ratio parameter $\beta$, (6.17) is modified according to

$$p'(\mathbf{c}'|\mathbf{c}) = \beta\frac{\Gamma(|\mathbf{c}'|+1)\Gamma(N)}{\Gamma(|\mathbf{c}'|+N)} + (1-\beta)p(\mathbf{c}'|\mathbf{c}) \tag{6.21}$$

and the distance function (6.20) is modified accordingly. As expected, the outlier part only depends on the number of drawn samples in $\mathbf{c}'$ and the number of bins.

Instead of the posterior predictive, we can also use a symmetric setting and use the divergence of the posterior distributions estimated from the two channel vectors; see Section 6.3.

# 6.3   COMPARING USING DIVERGENCES

In the previous section, we considered the posterior predictive to match a new channel vector $\mathbf{c}'$ to a previously observed vector $\mathbf{c}$. In symmetric settings, both channel vectors $\mathbf{c}$ and $\mathbf{c}'$ are drawn from the respective generating data distributions $p$ and $p'$. From these measurements, we now estimate the *divergences* of $p$ and $p'$. The Hellinger distance is a special case of the Hellinger divergence

$$H_\alpha(p\|p') = \frac{1}{\alpha - 1}\left(\int p(x)^\alpha p'(x)^{1-\alpha}\,\mathrm{d}x - 1\right) \tag{6.22}$$

for $\alpha = 1/2$. This and other special cases are listed in Table 6.1, in accordance with the classification of $\alpha$-divergences, as listed by Felsberg et al. [2013].

Table 6.1: Special cases of Hellinger divergences

| Case | Distance |
|---|---|
| $\alpha = 1/2$ | Hellinger distance |
| $\alpha \uparrow 1$ | Kullback-Leibler divergence |
| $\alpha \downarrow 0$ | Log-likelihood ratio |
| $\alpha = 2$ | Neyman $x^2$ divergence |
| $\alpha = -1$ | Pearson $x^2$ divergence |

Closely related to the Hellinger divergences are the Rényi divergences

$$R_\alpha(p\|p') = \frac{1}{\alpha - 1}\log\int p(x)^\alpha p'(x)^{1-\alpha}\,\mathrm{d}x \tag{6.23}$$

by the equality

$$H_\alpha(p\|p') = \frac{1}{\alpha - 1}(\exp((\alpha - 1)R_\alpha(p\|p')) - 1) \ . \tag{6.24}$$

Surprisingly, $\alpha \uparrow 1$ leads to the Kullback-Leibler divergence also in this case.

Moreover, for exponential families, closed form solutions of the Rényi divergence exist, in particular for the Dirichlet distribution (6.6). We obtain for a uniform prior $\alpha = 1$ (note that classical notation for both the Dirichlet prior and Rényi divergences makes use of $\alpha$; in what follows, $\alpha$ denotes the divergence parameter and the parameter of the Dirichlet distribution is set to 1):

$$R_\alpha(p(\mathbf{P}|\mathbf{c})\|p(\mathbf{P}|\mathbf{c}')) = \log\frac{B(\mathbf{c}')}{B(\mathbf{c})} + \frac{1}{\alpha - 1}\log\frac{B(\mathbf{c}_\alpha)}{B(\mathbf{c})}, \tag{6.25}$$

where $\mathbf{c}_\alpha = \alpha\mathbf{c} + (1 - \alpha)\mathbf{c}'$ and $B()$ is the $N$-dimensional Beta function as defined in the previous section.

Similarly, we can compute a closed form solution for the Hellinger divergence of Dirichlet distributions

$$H_\alpha(p(\mathbf{P}|\mathbf{c})\|p(\mathbf{P}|\mathbf{c}')) = \frac{1}{\alpha - 1}\left(\frac{B(\mathbf{c}')^{\alpha-1}B(\mathbf{c}_\alpha)}{B(\mathbf{c})^\alpha} - 1\right) \; , \tag{6.26}$$

but for numerical reasons, the Rényi divergence is preferable as it can be computed using log-Beta functions betaln()

$$R_\alpha(p(\mathbf{P}|\mathbf{c})\|p(\mathbf{P}|\mathbf{c}')) = \text{betaln}(\mathbf{c}') + \frac{1}{\alpha - 1}\text{betaln}(\mathbf{c}_\alpha) - \frac{\alpha}{\alpha - 1}\text{betaln}(\mathbf{c}) \; . \tag{6.27}$$

A further reason to prefer Rényi divergence over Hellinger divergence is the respective sensitivity to small perturbations. The derivative of the Hellinger divergence with respect to single channel coefficients scales with the divergence itself, which leads to a lack of robustness. In contrast,

$$\frac{\partial R_\alpha(p(\mathbf{P}|\mathbf{c})\|p(\mathbf{P}|\mathbf{c}'))}{\partial c_n'} = \psi(c_n') - \psi(|\mathbf{c}'|) + \psi(|\mathbf{c}_\alpha|) - \psi(c_{\alpha,n}) \; , \tag{6.28}$$

where $\psi(c_n) = \frac{\Gamma'(c_n)}{\Gamma(c_n)}$ is the digamma function, see, e.g., Van Trees et al. [2013, p. 104].

Thus, the Rényi divergences of the posteriors estimated from $\mathbf{c}$ and $\mathbf{c}'$ are candidates for suitable distance measures. Unfortunately, robustness against outliers is still limited and the introduction of an outlier process as in (6.25) is analytically cumbersome.

Also, the fully symmetric setting is less common in practice, but occurs, e.g., in the computation of affinity matrices for spectral clustering. Most cases aim at the comparison of a new measurement with previously acquired ones and the posterior predictive (6.25) is more suitable.

The proposed distances have been discussed assuming one-dimensional distributions, but the results generalize to higher dimensions, both for independent and dependent stochastic variables. Obviously, it is an advantage to have uniform marginals and for that case, dependent joint distributions correspond to a non-constant Copula distribution; see Section 6.4.

## 6.4   UNIFORMIZATION AND COPULA ESTIMATION

As mentioned in Section 6.1, we often assume a uniform prior for the channel vector. However, if we compute the marginal distribution from the posterior distribution for a large dataset, the components of a channel vector might be highly unbalanced. This issue can be addressed by placing channels in a non-regular way, according to the marginal distribution, i.e., with high channel density where samples are likely.

This placement is obtained by mapping samples using the cumulative density function of the distribution from which the samples are drawn. The cumulative density can be computed from the estimated distribution as obtained from maximum entropy decoding; see Section 5.3. The subsequent procedure has been proposed by Öfjäll and Felsberg [2017].

We start with the density function (5.20) (note $\lambda_0 = -\frac{3}{2}$) and obtain the cumulative density function

$$P(x) = \int_{-\infty}^{x} \frac{1}{3} \sum_{n=1}^{N} \lambda_n K(y - \xi_n) \, dy =$$

$$= \frac{1}{3} \sum_{n=1}^{N} \lambda_n \int_{-\infty}^{x} K(y - \xi_n) \, dy = \qquad (6.29)$$

$$= \frac{1}{3} \sum_{n=1}^{N} \lambda_n \hat{K}(x - \xi_n)$$

with the (cumulative) basis functions

$$\hat{K}(x) = \int_{-\infty}^{x} K(y) \, dy \ . \qquad (6.30)$$

Only three (for three overlapping channels) cumulative basis functions are in the transition region for any given $x$, (6.29) can thus be calculated in constant time (independent of channel count $N$) as

$$P(x) = \frac{1}{3} \sum_{n=j-1}^{j+1} \lambda_n \hat{K}(x - \xi_n) + \frac{N - (j + 1)}{N} \ , \qquad (6.31)$$

where $j$ is the central channel activated by $x$.

The function $P()$ maps values $x$ to the range $[0, 1]$. If the cumulative density function is accurately estimated, the mapped values will appear to be drawn from a uniform distribution. Thus, placing regularly spaced channels in this transformed space corresponds to a sample density dependent spacing in the original domain and leads to a uniform marginal distribution of the channel coefficients.

For multi-dimensional distributions, the mapped values can be used to estimate the Copula distribution. The Copula distribution estimates dependencies between dimensions by removing the effect of the marginal distributions. If the dimensions of a joint distribution are stochastically independent, the Copula is one. If the dimensions have a positive correlation coefficient, the Copula is larger than one, smaller otherwise.

Algorithmically, the estimate for the Copula density is obtained by encoding the mapped points using an outer product channel representation on the space $[0; 1] \times [0; 1]$. Figure 6.4 illustrates the process, with first estimating the marginal distributions and the respective cumulative functions that are then used to form the Copula estimation basis functions.

As an example, Copulas estimated from samples drawn from two different multivariate Gaussian distributions are shown in Figure 6.3. The covariance matrices of these distributions are, respectively,

$$\Sigma_1 = \begin{pmatrix} 0.3 & 0.3 \\ 0.3 & 1.2 \end{pmatrix} \quad \text{and} \quad \Sigma_2 = \begin{pmatrix} 0.3 & 0 \\ 0 & 1.2 \end{pmatrix}. \tag{6.32}$$

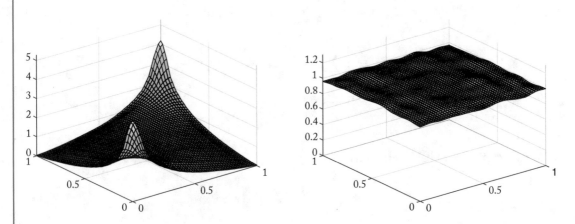

Figure 6.3: Copulas estimated from multivariate Gaussian distributions. Left: covariance $\Sigma_1$ (dependent); right: covariance $\Sigma_2$ (independent); see (6.32). Figure based on Öfjäll and Felsberg [2017].

In these estimated Copulas, the first 100 samples were only used for estimating the marginals. The subsequent samples were used both for updating the estimate of the marginals and for generating the Copula estimate. As apparent in the figures, the estimated Copula captures the dependency structure in the first case and the independence in the second case.

## SUMMARY

In this chapter we have discussed the comparison of channel representations based on their probabilistic interpretation. In asymmetric cases, the comparison can be done using the distance obtained from the posterior predictive, in symmetric cases by estimating the divergence of the two posterior distributions. Finally, the extension to dependent multi-dimensional distributions in terms Copula distributions has been discussed. The decomposition into marginals and Copula enable efficient schemes where the high-dimensional Copulas are only compared if the marginals already indicate a small distance.

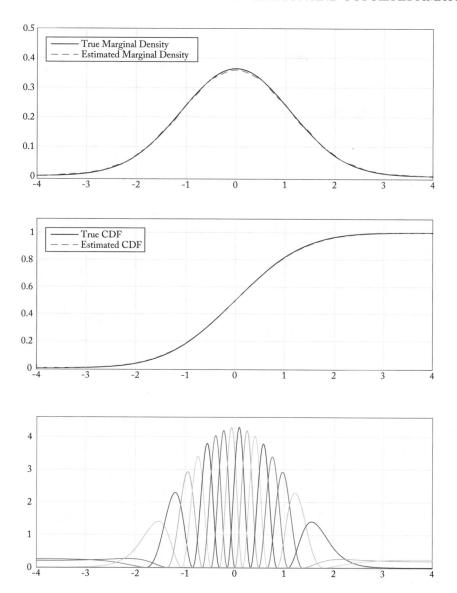

Figure 6.4: Top and middle: marginal density functions estimated using channel representations and maximum entropy reconstruction, compared with the true marginal densities. Bottom: basis functions for Copula estimation. The basis functions are regularly spaced on [0; 1] and mapped back to the original domain using the inverse estimated cumulative function. When estimating the Copula, samples are instead mapped by the estimated cumulative function. Figure based on Öfjäll and Felsberg [2017].

CHAPTER 7

# Conclusions

This book summarizes work on channel representations from dozens of publications over a period of about 20 years. The purpose of this summary has not been to conclude the work on channel representations and to produce a comprehensive review of all details, but to illustrate the use of the channel representation as a mathematical and algorithmic tool.

In the area of deep learning, many researchers work on topics about feature representations, biologically motivated, or based on probabilistic modeling. With its connection to computational neuroscience and probability and estimation theory, channel representations are a useful example for those researchers.

The connections to popular feature descriptors in 2D and 3D, including their visualization, makes the channel representation a universal toolbox for the practitioner. With its connection to orientation scores, population codes, and average shifted histograms, channel representation embed well in other related topics.

The probabilistic modeling, the Bayesian viewpoint, and the probabilistic distance measures are applicable to many other, similar cases, too. Together with the code from the repositories at `https://github.com/micfe03/channel_representation`, hopefully many users will find this text useful for their research work and apply the estimation methods in their regression or classification problems.

To this end, it is worthwhile mentioning that a connection also exists between channel representations and discrete, or symbolic, spaces. In a sense, the normalized channel representation can be seen as a kind of softmax function that helps to map from linear spaces to categorical spaces.

In this way, the channel representation becomes a universal representation for both continuous spaces and regression problems as well as for discrete spaces and classification problems.

# Bibliography

Bay, H., Ess, A., Tuytelaars, T., and Van Gool, L. [2008]. Speeded-up robust features (surf), *Computer Vision and Image Understanding*, **110**(3), pp. 346–359. http://dx.doi.org/10.1016/j.cviu.2007.09.014 DOI: 10.1016/j.cviu.2007.09.014. 11, 43

Bekkers, E., Duits, R., Berendschot, T., and ter Haar Romeny, B. [2014]. A multi-orientation analysis approach to retinal vessel tracking, *Journal of Mathematical Imaging and Vision*, **49**(3), pp. 583–610. https://doi.org/10.1007/s10851-013-0488-6 DOI: 10.1007/s10851-013-0488-6. 25

Bishop, C. M. [1995]. *Neural Networks for Pattern Recognition*, Oxford University Press, New York. 12, 20

Bosking, W. H., Zhang, Y., Schofield, B., and Fitzpatrick, D. [1997]. Orientation selectivity and the arrangement of horizontal connections in tree shrew striate cortex, *Journal of Neuroscience*, **17**(6), pp. 2112–2127. http://www.jneurosci.org/content/17/6/2112 DOI: 10.1523/jneurosci.17-06-02112.1997. 16

Burkhardt, H. [1989]. Homogeneous Structures for Position-Invariant Feature Extraction, in J. C. Simon, Ed., *From the Pixels to the Features*, COST 13 Workshop, Bonas (F), North-Holland, August 1988. 8

Dalal, N. and Triggs, B. [2005]. Histograms of oriented gradients for human detection, in *Computer Vision and Pattern Recognition (CVPR), IEEE Computer Society Conference on*, Vol. 1, pp. 886–893. DOI: 10.1109/cvpr.2005.177. 12, 34, 35, 36, 37

Danelljan, M., Bhat, G., Khan, F. S., and Felsberg, M. [2017]. ECO: Efficient convolution operators for tracking, in *CVPR*, Vol. abs/1611.09224. http://arxiv.org/abs/1611.09224 DOI: 10.1109/cvpr.2017.733. 10

Danelljan, M., Häger, G., Khan, F. S., and Felsberg, M. [2015]. Coloring channel representations for visual tracking, in *SCIA*. DOI: 10.1007/978-3-319-19665-7_10. 21

Danelljan, M., Meneghetti, G., Shahbaz Khan, F., and Felsberg, M. [2016]. A probabilistic framework for color-based point set registration, in *CVPR*. DOI: 10.1109/cvpr.2016.201. 23, 24 d'Angelo, E., Alahi, A., and Vandergheynst, P. [2012]. Beyond bits: Reconstructing images from local binary descriptors, in *Pattern Recognition (ICPR), 21st International Conference on*, pp. 935–938. 54

Denève, S., Latham, P. E., and Pouget, A. [1999]. Reading population codes: A neural implementation of ideal observers, *Nature Neuroscience*, **2**(8), pp. 740–745. DOI: 10.1038/11205. 11, 15

Denève, S., Latham, P. E., and Pouget, A. [2001]. Efficient computation and cue integration with noisy population codes, *Nature Neuroscience*, **4**(8), pp. 826–831. DOI: 10.1038/90541. 15

Duits, R., Duits, M., van Almsick, M., and ter Haar Romeny, B. [2007]. Invertible orientation scores as an application of generalized wavelet theory, *Pattern Recognition and Image Analysis*, **17**(1), pp. 42–75. https://doi.org/10.1134/S1054661807010063 DOI: 10.1134/s105466180703011x. 23, 24, 25

Duits, R., Felsberg, M., and Florack, L. M. J. [2003]. $\alpha$ scale spaces on a bounded domain, in L. D. Griffin and M. Lillholm, Eds., Scale Space'03, Vol. 2695 of *LNCS*, Springer, Heidelberg, pp. 494–510. 10

Duits, R., Felsberg, M., Granlund, G. H., and ter Haar Romeny, B. M. [2007]. Image analysis and reconstruction using a wavelet transform constructed from a reducible representation of the Euclidean motion group, *International Journal of Computer Vision*, **72**(1), pp. 79–102. DOI: 10.1007/s11263-006-8894-5. 23, 24, 57

Duits, R. and Franken, E. [2010]. Left-invariant parabolic evolutions on SE(2) and contour enhancement via invertible orientation scores Part II: Nonlinear left-invariant diffusions on invertible orientation scores, *Quarterly of Applied Mathematics*, **68**(2), pp. 293–331. http://dx.doi.org/10.1090/S0033-569X-10-01173-3 DOI: 10.1090/s0033-569x-10-01173-3. 9

Evans, M., Hastings, N., and Peacock, J. B. [2000]. *Statistical Distributions*, 3rd ed., Wiley-Interscience. 57, 58, 62

Farnebäck, G. [1999]. Spatial domain methods for orientation and velocity estimation, Lic. Thesis LiU-Tek-Lic-1999:13, Dept. EE, Linköping University. 39

Felsberg, M. [1998]. Signal processing using frequency domain methods in Clifford algebra, Diploma thesis, Institute of Computer Science and Applied Mathematics, Christian-Albrechts-University of Kiel. xi

Felsberg, M. [2002]. *Low-Level Image Processing with the Structure Multivector*, Ph.D. thesis, Institute of Computer Science and Applied Mathematics, Christian-Albrechts-University of Kiel. www.informatik.uni-kiel.de/reports/2002/0203.html 2, 35

Felsberg, M. [2005]. Wiener channel smoothing: Robust Wiener filtering of images, in *DAGM*, Vol. 3663 of *LNCS*, Springer, pp. 468–475. DOI: 10.1007/11550518_58. 48

Felsberg, M. [2009]. Spatio-featural scale-space, in *International Conference on Scale Space Methods and Variational Methods in Computer Vision*, Vol. 5567 of *LNCS*. DOI: 10.1007/978-3-642-02256-2_67. 34

Felsberg, M. [2010]. Incremental computation of feature hierarchies, in *Pattern Recognition, Proceedings of the 32nd DAGM*. DOI: 10.1007/978-3-642-15986-2_53. 14, 32, 33, 34, 35

Felsberg, M. [2011]. Autocorrelation-driven diffusion filtering, *IEEE Transactions on Image Processing*, **20**(7). DOI: 10.1109/tip.2011.2107330. 10

Felsberg, M. [2013]. Enhanced distribution field tracking using channel representations, in *IEEE ICCV Workshop on Visual Object Tracking Challenge*. DOI: 10.1109/iccvw.2013.22. 12, 21, 22, 60, 61

Felsberg, M., Forssén, P.-E., and Scharr, H. [2006]. Channel smoothing: Efficient robust smoothing of low-level signal features, *IEEE Transactions on Pattern Analysis and Machine Intelligence*, **28**(2), pp. 209–222. DOI: 10.1109/tpami.2006.29. 14, 18, 46, 47, 48, 53, 57

Felsberg, M. and Granlund, G. [2003]. Anisotropic channel filtering, in *Proc. 13th Scandinavian Conference on Image Analysis LNCS*, 2749, pp. 755–762. DOI: 10.1007/3-540-45103-x_100. 29, 45, 48

Felsberg, M. and Granlund, G. [2004]. POI detection using channel clustering and the 2D energy tensor, in *26th DAGM Symposium Mustererkennung, Tübingen*. DOI: 10.1007/978-3-540-28649-3_13. 48

Felsberg, M. and Granlund, G. [2006]. P-channels: Robust multivariate m-estimation of large datasets, in *International Conference on Pattern Recognition*, Hong Kong. DOI: 10.1109/icpr.2006.911. 12, 28, 29, 37

Felsberg, M. and Hedborg, J. [2007a]. Real-time view-based pose recognition and interpolation for tracking initialization, *Journal of Real-Time Image Processing*, **2**(2–3), pp. 103–116. DOI: 10.1007/s11554-007-0044-y. 14, 37

Felsberg, M. and Hedborg, J. [2007b]. Real-time visual recognition of objects and scenes using p-channel matching, in *Proc. 15th Scandinavian Conference on Image Analysis*, Vol. 4522 of *LNCS*, pp. 908–917. DOI: 10.1007/978-3-540-73040-8_92. 28, 29, 39, 40

Felsberg, M., Kalkan, S., and Krüger, N. [2009]. Continuous dimensionality characterization of image structures, *Image and Vision Computing*, **27**(6), pp. 628–636. DOI: 10.1016/j.imavis.2008.06.018. 58

Felsberg, M., Larsson, F., Wiklund, J., Wadstromer, N., and Ahlberg, J. [2013]. Online learning of correspondences between images, *Pattern Analysis and Machine Intelligence, IEEE Transactions on*, **35**(1), pp. 118–129. DOI: 10.1109/tpami.2012.65. 32, 63

Felsberg, M., Öfjäll, K., and Lenz, R. [2015]. Unbiased decoding of biologically motivated visual feature descriptors, *Frontiers in Robotics and AI*, **2**(20). DOI: 10.3389/frobt.2015.00020. 11, 14, 16, 21, 46, 48, 49, 50

Felsberg, M. and Sommer, G. [2001]. The monogenic signal, *IEEE Transactions on Signal Processing*, **49**(12), pp. 3136–3144. DOI: 10.1109/78.969520. 9

Ferraro, M. and Caelli, T. M. [1994]. Lie transformation groups, integral transforms, and invariant pattern recognition, *Spatial Vision*, **8**(4), pp. 33–44. DOI: 10.1163/156856894x00224. 9

Forssén, P.-E. [2004]. *Low and Medium Level Vision using Channel Representations*, Ph.D. thesis, Linköping University, Sweden. 14, 18, 19, 46, 47, 48

Förstner, W. [1991]. *Statistische Verfahren für die automatische Bildanalyse und ihre Bewertung bei der Objekterkennung und -vermessung*, number 370 in C, Verlag der Bayerischen Akademie der Wissenschaften. 7

Freeman, W. T. and Adelson, E. H. [1991]. The design and use of steerable filters, *IEEE Transactions on Pattern Analysis and Machine Intelligent*, **13**(9), pp. 891–906. DOI: 10.1109/34.93808. 10

Goodfellow, I., Bengio, Y., and Courville, A. [2016]. *Deep Learning*, MIT Press. http://www.deeplearningbook.org 2, 9

Granlund, G. [2000a]. *The Dichotomy of Strategies for Spatial-Cognitive Information Processing*, Other academic LiTH-ISY-R, 2241, Linköping University, Department of Electrical Engineering, Sweden. 10

Granlund, G. H. [1972]. Fourier preprocessing for hand print character recognition, *IEEE Transactions on Computers*, **C–21**(2), pp. 195–201. DOI: 10.1109/tc.1972.5008926. 8

Granlund, G. H. [1999]. The complexity of vision, *Signal Processing*, **74**(1), pp. 101–126. DOI: 10.1016/s0165-1684(98)00204-7. 2, 14

Granlund, G. H. [2000b]. An associative perception-action structure using a localized space variant information representation, in *Proc. of Algebraic Frames for the Perception–Action Cycle (AFPAC)*, Kiel, Germany. DOI: 10.1007/10722492_3. 14, 27, 39, 57

Granlund, G. H. and Knutsson, H. [1995]. *Signal Processing for Computer Vision*, Kluwer Academic Publishers, Dordrecht. DOI: 10.1007/978-1-4757-2377-9. 2, 3, 4, 8, 9

Gross, R., Matthews, I., Cohn, J., Kanade, T., and Baker, S. [2010]. Multi-pie, *Image and Vision Computing*, **28**(5), pp. 807–813. Best of Automatic Face and Gesture Recognition 2008. http://www.sciencedirect.com/science/article/pii/S0262885609001711 DOI: 10.1016/j.imavis.2009.08.002. 32

Guo, Y., Sohel, F., Bennamoun, M., Lu, M., and Wan, J. [2013]. Rotational projection statistics for 3D local surface description and object recognition, *International Journal of Computer Vision*, **105**(1), pp. 63–86. https://doi.org/10.1007/s11263-013-0627-y DOI: 10.1007/s11263-013-0627-y. 41, 43

Harris, C. G. and Stephens, M. [1988]. A combined corner and edge detector, in *4th Alvey Vision Conference*, pp. 147–151. DOI: 10.5244/c.2.23. 7

Howard, I. P. and Rogers, B. J. [1995]. *Binocular Vision and Stereopsis*, Oxford University Press, Oxford, UK. DOI: 10.1093/acprof:oso/9780195084764.001.0001. 15

Huang, D., Cabral, R. S., and De la Torre, F. [2012]. Robust regression, in *European Conference on Computer Vision (ECCV)*. DOI: 10.1007/978-3-642-33765-9_44. 32

Hubel, D. H. and Wiesel, T. N. [1959]. Receptive fields of single neurones in the cat's striate cortex, *The Journal of Physiology*, **148**(3), pp. 574–591. http://jp.physoc.org/content/148/3/574.short DOI: 10.1113/jphysiol.1959.sp006308. 15

Hutter, M. [2013]. Sparse adaptive dirichlet-multinomial-like processes, in S. Shalev-Shwartz and I. Steinwart, Eds, *COLT*, Vol. 30 of *JMLR Workshop and Conference Proceedings*, pp. 432–459. 59

Jähne, B. [2005]. *Digital Image Processing*, 6th ed., Springer, Berlin. DOI: 10.1007/3-540-27563-0. 35

Johansson, B. [2004]. *Low Level Operations and Learning in Computer Vision*, Ph.D. thesis, Linköping University, Linköping, Sweden. Dissertation No. 912, 34

Johansson, B., Elfving, T., Kozlov, V., Censor, Y., Forssén, P.-E., and Granlund, G. [2006]. The application of an oblique-projected landweber method to a model of supervised learning, *Mathematical and Computer Modelling*, **43**, pp. 892–909. DOI: 10.1016/j.mcm.2005.12.010. 31

Jonsson, E. [2008]. *Channel-Coded Feature Maps for Computer Vision and Machine Learning*, Ph.D. thesis, Linköping University, Linköping, Sweden. Dissertation No. 1160, 27, 31, 32, 37, 38, 61

Jonsson, E. and Felsberg, M. [2005]. Reconstruction of probability density functions from channel representations, in *Proc. 14th Scandinavian Conference on Image Analysis*. DOI: 10.1007/11499145_50. 17, 47, 50, 51, 52

Jonsson, E. and Felsberg, M. [2007]. Accurate interpolation in appearance-based pose estimation, in *Proc. 15th Scandinavian Conference on Image Analysis*, Vol. 4522 of *LNCS*, pp. 1–10. DOI: 10.1007/978-3-540-73040-8_1. 37

Jonsson, E. and Felsberg, M. [2009]. Efficient computation of channel-coded feature maps through piecewise polynomials, *Image and Vision Computing*, **27**(11), pp. 1688–1694. DOI: 10.1016/j.imavis.2008.11.002. 14, 29, 31, 32

Kanatani, K., Sugaya, Y., and Kanazawa, Y. [2016]. Ellipse fitting for computer vision: Implementation and applications, *Synthesis Lectures on Computer Vision*, **6**(1), pp. 1–141. http://dx.doi.org/10.2200/S00713ED1V01Y201603COV008 DOI: 10.2200/s00713ed1v01y201603cov008. 7

Kass, M. and Solomon, J. [2010]. Smoothed local histogram filters, in *ACM SIGGRAPH Papers*, New York, pp. 100:1–100:10. http://doi.acm.org/10.1145/1833349.1778837 DOI: 10.1145/1833349.1778837. 47

Kato, H. and Harada, T. [2014]. Image reconstruction from bag-of-visual-words, in *Computer Vision and Pattern Recognition (CVPR), IEEE Conference on*, pp. 955–962. DOI: 10.1109/cvpr.2014.127. 54

Khan, F. S., van de Weijer, J., Ali, S., and Felsberg, M. [2013]. Evaluating the impact of color on texture recognition, in R. C. Wilson, E. R. Hancock, A. G. Bors, and W. A. P. Smith, Eds., CAIP (1), Vol. 8047 of *Lecture Notes in Computer Science*, pp. 154–162, Springer. DOI: 10.1007/978-3-642-40261-6. 27

Knopp, J., Prasad, M., Willems, G., Timofte, R., and Van Gool, L. [2010]. *Hough Transform and 3D-SURF for Robust Three-Dimensional Classification*, Springer Berlin Heidelberg, Berlin, Heidelberg, pp. 589–602. DOI: 10.1007/978-3-642-15567-3_43. 11, 43

Knutsson, H., Wilson, R., and Granlund, G. H. [1983]. Anisotropic non-stationary image estimation and its applications: Part I—restoration of noisy images, *IEEE Transactions on Communications*, **COM–31**(3), pp. 388–397. DOI: 10.1109/tcom.1983.1095832. 10

Koenderink, J. J. [1993]. What is a feature?, *Journal of Intelligent Systems*, **3**(1), pp. 49–82. DOI: 10.1515/jisys.1993.3.1.49. 1, 8

Koenderink, J. J. and van Doorn, A. J. [2002]. Image processing done right, in *Proc. European Conference on Computer Vision*, pp. 158–172. DOI: 10.1007/3-540-47969-4_11. xi, 1, 14, 34

Kristan, M., Leonardis, A., Matas, J., Felsberg, M., Pflugfelder, R., and et al. [2016]. The visual object tracking VOT challenge results, in *ECCV Workshop Proceedings*. 21

Kristan, M., Matas, J., Leonardis, A., Vojir, T., Pflugfelder, R., Fernandez, G., Nebehay, G., Porikli, F., and Čehovin, L. [2016]. A novel performance evaluation methodology for single-target trackers, *IEEE Transactions on Pattern Analysis and Machine Intelligence*. DOI: 10.1109/tpami.2016.2516982. 8

Larsson, F., Felsberg, M., and Forssén, P.-E. [2011]. Correlating Fourier descriptors of local patches for road sign recognition, *IET Computer Vision*, **5**(4), pp. 244–254. DOI: 10.1049/iet-cvi.2010.0040. 9

Lenz, R., Carmona, P. L., and Meer, P. [2007]. The hyperbolic geometry of illumination-induced chromaticity changes, in *Computer Vision and Pattern Recognition*, pp. 1–6. DOI: 10.1109/cvpr.2007.383212. 14

Liaw, A. and Wiener, M. [2002]. Classification and regression by randomforest, *R News*, **2**(3), pp. 18–22. 32

Lowe, D. G. [2004]. Distinctive image features from scale-invariant keypoints, *International Journal of Computer Vision*, **60**(2), pp. 91–110. DOI: 10.1023/b:visi.0000029664.99615.94. 12, 34, 38, 46

Lüdtke, N. L., Wilson, R. C., and Hancock, E. R. [2002]. Probabilistic population coding of multiple edge orientation, in *Proc. of IEEE International Conference on Image Processing*, Vol. II, pp. 865–868. DOI: 10.1109/icip.2002.1040088. 14

Mahendran, A. and Vedaldi, A. [2015]. Understanding deep image representations by inverting them, in *The IEEE Conference on Computer Vision and Pattern Recognition (CVPR)*. DOI: 10.1109/cvpr.2015.7299155. 54

Mallat, S. [2016]. Understanding deep convolutional networks, *Philosophical Transactions of the Royal Society of London A: Mathematical, Physical and Engineering Sciences*, **374**(2065). http://rsta.royalsocietypublishing.org/content/374/2065/20150203 DOI: 10.1098/rsta.2015.0203. xi, 2, 8, 9

Mallat, S. G. [1989]. A theory for multiresolution signal decomposition: The wavelet representation, *IEEE Transactions on Pattern Analysis and Machine Intelligence*, **11**, pp. 674–693. DOI: 10.1109/34.192463. 23

Marr, D. [1982]. *Vision: A Computational Investigation into the Human Representation and Processing of Visual Information*, Henry Holt and Co., Inc., New York. DOI: 10.7551/mitpress/9780262514620.001.0001. 1

Nordberg, K. and Granlund, G. [1996]. Equivariance and Invariance—An Approach Based on Lie Groups, in *ICIP*. DOI: 10.1109/icip.1996.560414. 9

Nordberg, K., Granlund, G. H., and Knutsson, H. [1994]. Representation and learning of invariance, in *Proc. of IEEE International Conference on Image Processing*. DOI: 10.1109/icip.1994.413638. 12, 14, 21

Öfjäll, K. and Felsberg, M. [2014a]. Biologically inspired online learning of visual autonomous driving, in *BMVC*. DOI: 10.5244/c.28.94. 32, 33

Öfjäll, K. and Felsberg, M. [2014b]. Weighted update and comparison for channel-based distribution field tracking, in *ECCV Workshop on Visual Object Tracking Challenge*. DOI: 10.1007/978-3-319-16181-5_15. 22, 23, 50

Öfjäll, K. and Felsberg, M. [2017]. Approximative coding methods for channel representations, *Journal of Mathematical Imaging and Vision*. DOI: 10.1007/s10851-017-0775-8. 13, 26, 42, 51, 54, 64, 66, 67

Olshausen, B. A. and Field, D. J. [1997]. Sparse coding with an overcomplete basis set: A strategy employed by v1?, *Vision Research*, **37**(23), pp. 3311–3325. http://www.sciencedirect.com/science/article/pii/S0042698997001697 DOI: 10.1016/s0042-6989(97)00169-7. 15, 55

Pagani, A., Stricker, D., and Felsberg, M. [2009]. Integral P-channels for fast and robust region matching, in *ICIP*. DOI: 10.1109/icip.2009.5414467. 28

Papert, S. A. [1966]. The summer vision project, MIT, AI memos. http://hdl.handle.net/1721.1/6125 1

Paris, S. and Durand, F. [2006]. A fast approximation of the bilateral filter using a signal processing approach, in *European Conference on Computer Vision*. DOI: 10.1007/11744085_44. 47

Philbin, J., Chum, O., Isard, M., Sivic, J., and Zisserman, A. [2007]. Object retrieval with large vocabularies and fast spatial matching, in *IEEE Conference on Computer Vision and Pattern Recognition*, pp. 1–8. DOI: 10.1109/cvpr.2007.383172. 12

Pouget, A., Dayan, P., and Zemel, R. [2000]. Information processing with population codes, *Nature Reviews–Neuroscience*, **1**, pp. 125–132. DOI: 10.1038/35039062. 12

Pouget, A., Dayan, P., and Zemel, R. S. [2003]. Inference and computation with population codes, *Annual Review of Neuroscience*, **26**, pp. 381–410. DOI: 10.1146/annurev.neuro.26.041002.131112. 14

Rao, R. P. N. and Ballard, D. H. [1999]. Predictive coding in the visual cortex: A functional interpretation of some extra-classical receptive-field effects, *Nature Neuroscience*, **2**(1), pp. 79–87. DOI: 10.1038/4580. 15

Riesenhuber, M. and Poggio, T. [1999]. Hierarchical models of object recognition in cortex, *Nature Neuroscience*, **2**(11), pp. 1019–1025. http://dx.doi.org/10.1038/14819 DOI: 10.1038/14819. 15

Rodehorst, V. and Koschan, A. [2006]. Comparison and evaluation of feature point detectors, in L. Gründig and M. O. Altan, Eds., *Proc. of the 5th International Symposium—Turkish-German Joint Geodetic Days (TGJGD)*, pp. 1–8, Berlin. http://rodehorst.info/web/html/img/pool/TGJGD06.pdf 7

Russakovsky, O., Deng, J., Su, H., Krause, J., Satheesh, S., Ma, S., Huang, Z., Karpathy, A., Khosla, A., Bernstein, M. et al. [2014]. Imagenet large scale visual recognition challenge, *arXiv preprint arXiv:1409.0575*. DOI: 10.1007/s11263-015-0816-y. xi

Rusu, R. B., Blodow, N., and Beetz, M. [2009]. Fast point feature histograms (FPFH) for 3D registration, in *IEEE International Conference on Robotics and Automation*, pp. 3212–3217. DOI: 10.1109/robot.2009.5152473. 11

Sabour, S., Frosst, N., and Hinton, G. E. [2017]. Dynamic routing between capsules, in *Advances in Neural Information Processing Systems 30th Annual Conference on Neural Information Processing Systems*, pp. 3859–3869, Long Beach, CA. http://papers.nips.cc/paper/6975-dynamic-routing-between-capsules 15

Salti, S., Tombari, F., and Stefano, L. D. [2014]. Shot: Unique signatures of histograms for surface and texture description, *Computer Vision and Image Understanding*, **125**, pp. 251–264. http://www.sciencedirect.com/science/article/pii/S1077314214000988 DOI: 10.1016/j.cviu.2014.04.011. 11, 41, 42, 43

Sánchez, J., Perronnin, F., Mensink, T., and Verbeek, J. [2013]. Image classification with the fisher vector: Theory and practice, *International Journal of Computer Vision*, **105**(3), pp. 222–245. http://dx.doi.org/10.1007/s11263-013-0636-x DOI: 10.1007/s11263-013-0636-x. 12, 61

Scharr, H., Körkel, S., and Jähne, B. [1997]. *Numerische Isotropieoptimierung von FIR-Filtern mittels Querglättung*, in E. Paulus and F. M. Wahl, Eds., *19th DAGM Symposium Mustererkennung, Braunschweig*, pp. 367–374. 10

Schmid, C., Mohr, R., and Bauckhage, C. [2000]. Evaluation of interest point detectors, *International Journal of Computer Vision*, **37**(2), pp. 151–172. DOI: 10.1007/978-3-642-60893-3_39. 7

Scott, D. [1992]. *Multivariate Density Estimation: Theory, Practice, and Visualization*, Wiley Series in Probability and Statistics, Wiley. DOI: 10.1002/9781118575574. 59

Scott, D. W. [1985]. Averaged shifted histograms: Effective nonparametric density estimators in several dimensions, *Annals of Statistics*, **13**(3), pp. 1024–1040. DOI: 10.1214/aos/1176349654. 14

Sevilla-Lara, L. and Learned-Miller, E. [2012]. Distribution fields for tracking, in *Computer Vision and Pattern Recognition (CVPR), IEEE Conference on*, pp. 1910–1917. DOI: 10.1109/cvpr.2012.6247891. 12, 21, 22, 46, 60

Sharma, U. and Duits, R. [2015]. Left-invariant evolutions of wavelet transforms on the similitude group, *Applied and Computational Harmonic Analysis*, **39**(1), pp. 110–137. http://www.sciencedirect.com/science/article/pii/S1063520314001171    DOI: 10.1016/j.acha.2014.09.001. 26

Sivic, J. and Zisserman, A. [2003]. Video google: A text retrieval approach to object matching in videos, in *Proc. 9th IEEE International Conference on Computer Vision*, Vol. 2, pp. 1470–1477. DOI: 10.1109/iccv.2003.1238663. 11

Snippe, H. P. and Koenderink, J. J. [1992]. Discrimination thresholds for channel-coded systems, *Biological Cybernetics*, **66**, pp. 543–551. DOI: 10.1007/bf00204120. 12, 14

Spies, H. and Forssén, P.-E. [2003]. Two-dimensional channel representation for multiple velocities, in *Proc. of the 13th Scandinavian Conference on Image Analysis LNCS*, 2749, pp. 356–362, Gothenburg, Sweden. DOI: 10.1007/3-540-45103-x_49. 27

Thorpe, S. [2002]. Ultra-rapid scene categorisation with a wave of spikes, in *Biologically Motivated Computer Vision*, Vol. 2525 of *LNCS*, Springer Berlin. DOI: 10.1007/3-540-36181-2_1. 15

Van De Weijer, J., Schmid, C., Verbeek, J., and Larlus, D. [2009]. Learning color names for real-world applications, *Image Processing, IEEE Transactions on*, **18**(7), pp. 1512–1523. DOI: 10.1109/tip.2009.2019809. 14, 28, 39

Van Trees, H., Bell, K., and Tian, Z. [2013]. *Detection Estimation and Modulation Theory, Part I: Detection, Estimation, and Filtering Theory*, Detection Estimation and Modulation Theory, Wiley. https://books.google.se/books?id=dnvaxqHDkbQC DOI: 10.1002/0471221090. 64

Vedaldi, A. and Fulkerson, B. [2008]. VLFeat: An open and portable library of computer vision algorithms. http://www.vlfeat.org/ DOI: 10.1145/1873951.1874249. 38

Vondrick, C., Khosla, A., Malisiewicz, T., and Torralba, A. [2013]. HOGgles: Visualizing object detection features, *ICCV*. DOI: 10.1109/iccv.2013.8. 54, 55

Wallenberg, M., Felsberg, M., Forssen, P.-E., and Dellen, B. [2011]. Channel coding for joint colour and depth segmentation, in *Proc. of Pattern Recognition 33rd DAGM Symposium*, Frankfurt/Main, Germany, August 31–September 2, Vol. 6835 of *Lecture Notes in Computer Science*, pp. 306–315, SpringerLink. DOI: 10.1007/978-3-642-23123-0_31. 27, 28

Weickert, J. [1996]. *Anisotropic Diffusion in Image Processing*, Ph.D. thesis, Faculty of Mathematics, University of Kaiserslautern. 10

Weinzaepfel, P., Jegou, H., and Perez, P. [2011]. Reconstructing an image from its local descriptors, in *Computer Vision and Pattern Recognition (CVPR), IEEE Conference on*, pp. 337–344. DOI: 10.1109/cvpr.2011.5995616. 54, 55

Zaharescu, A., Boyer, E., and Horaud, R. [2012]. Keypoints and local descriptors of scalar functions on 2D manifolds, *International Journal of Computer Vision*, **100**(1), pp. 78–98. https://doi.org/10.1007/s11263-012-0528-5 DOI: 10.1007/s11263-012-0528-5. 41, 43

Zeiler, M. and Fergus, R. [2014]. Visualizing and understanding convolutional networks, in D. Fleet, T. Pajdla, B. Schiele, and T. Tuytelaars, Eds., *Computer Vision (ECCV)*, Vol. 8689 of *Lecture Notes in Computer Science*, pp. 818–833, Springer International Publishing. http://dx.doi.org/10.1007/978-3-319-10590-1_53 DOI: 10.1007/978-3-319-10590-1. 54

Zemel, R. S., Dayan, P., and Pouget, A. [1998]. Probabilistic interpretation of population codes, *Neural Computation*, **10**(2), pp. 403–430. DOI: 10.1162/089976698300017818. 12

# Author's Biography

## MICHAEL FELSBERG

**Michael Felsberg** received the Ph.D. in engineering from the University of Kiel, Germany, in 2002. Since 2008, he has been a Full Professor and the Head of the Computer Vision Laboratory at Linköping University, Sweden. His current research interests include signal processing methods for image analysis, computer and robot vision, and machine learning. He has published more than 150 reviewed conference papers, journal articles, and book contributions.

He was a recipient of awards from the German Pattern Recognition Society in 2000, 2004, and 2005, from the Swedish Society for Automated Image Analysis in 2007 and 2010, from the Conference on Information Fusion in 2011 (Honorable Mention), from the CVPR Workshop on Mobile Vision 2014, and from the ICPR 2016 track on Computer Vision (Best Paper). He has achieved top ranks on various challenges (VOT: 3rd 2013, 1st 2014, 2nd 2015, 1st 2016, 1st 2017 (sequestered test); VOT-TIR: 1st 2015, 1st 2016, 3rd 2017; OpenCV Tracking: 1st 2015; KITTI Stereo Odometry: 1st 2015, March).

He has coordinated the EU projects COSPAL and DIPLECS and has been an Associate Editor of the *Journal of Mathematical Imaging and Vision* and the *Journal of Image and Vision Computing*. He was Publication Chair of the International Conference on Pattern Recognition 2014 and served as Track Chair in 2016, has been a VOT-committee member since 2015, was the General Co-Chair of the DAGM symposium in 2011 and General Chair of CAIP 2017, and will be Area Chair at ECCV 2018 and Program Chair of SCIA 2019.

# Index

Printed in the United States
by Baker & Taylor Publisher Services